THE SHOOTING OF MICHAEL COLLINS

THE SHOOTING

OF

MICHAEL COLLINS

MURDER OR ACCIDENT?

JOHN M. FEEHAN

Truth is the shattered mirror strown
In myriad bits;
While each believes his little bit
*   The whole to own.*
                    SIR RICHARD BURTON

Royal Carbery Books

ROYAL CARBERY BOOKS
36 Beechwood Park, Ballinlough, Cork

Trade Distributors:
MERCIER PRESS
PO Box 5, 5 French Church Street, Cork
16 Hume Street, Dublin 2

ISBN 0 946645 03 5

First published June 1981
Reprinted July 1981
Revised edition, April 1982
Reprinted 1987, 1988, 1989
Revised edition 1991

10 9 8 7 6 5 4 3 2

DEDICATED TO
Johanna and Brendan O'Reilly

The author would like to acknowledge with thanks the helpfulness and courtesy of the staffs of the City and County Libraries, Cork, the staff of the UCD Archives, Stephen's Green, Dublin, and the National library.

Printed in Ireland by Colour Books Ltd.

Contents

Preface to the Sixth Edition

It is now ten years since the first edition of this book was published and in the intervening period all kinds of theories, ideas, and opinions have been expressed as to how Collins met his death. Nothing has been said or written, however, that would cause me to change in any way the conclusions I expressed in the last chapters of this book.

As this edition was going to press a new biography of Michael Collins by Tim Pat Coogan was published. It is a good book – well balanced, well researched and well written.

Despite its excellence, however, I do not agree with his views on the death of Collins and its aftermath. I believe the account in this book comes nearer to what actually happened.

I have written a new Epilogue: *Did Sonny O'Neill Shoot Michael Collins?* I have done so in the interests of historical accuracy. This epilogue fully explains itself.

I would like to record with regret the death of William McKenna of Athlone, the last remaining member of the Collins escort, who gave me much help in assembling the facts of the ambush, by placing at my disposal valuable documents, and by giving me a minute-by-minute account of what happened on the Free State side. May he rest in peace.

J.M.F

Introduction

There is a story told about a television producer who made a four-part film on some aspect of the First World War. When this film was transmitted he received so many letters from people who had important and relevant information that he had to remake it, this time in sixteen parts, in order to adequately cover all its different and more up-to-date aspects.

I feel somewhat akin to that film producer. When this book was first published in June 1981 it sold out in a few weeks and the second printing was exhausted almost as quickly. I was on the point of printing for the third time, but on reflection decided not to do so immediately as the amount of fresh and useful information which came my way made a complete re-writing of certain sections necessary.

Hundreds of people contacted me by letter, telephone and personal call, and what they had to say was most pertinent and valuable. Quite a few spoke more freely and more openly than normal because they knew that I would not reveal any of my sources without permission. Although this may be irritating to historians it certainly makes for far better and more accurate history. In the grey misty area of possible political murder the best sources are the people who have some first-hand, or even second-hand, knowledge of what happened. Killers do not write memos to be put on file for the benefit of scholars, nor do secret service men carry placards announcing their profession to all and sundry. Those who gave information in this area understandably prefer to remain anonymous.

I am afraid that I grossly under-estimated the eagerness of certain people to put words into my mouth which I never uttered and to suggest implications which simply

7

did not exist. I think it is clear to any fair-minded reader that this book does not try to prove that Collins was murdered. It only raises some awkward and probing questions, many of which have been brushed under the carpet in the past. I need hardly emphasise that I do not know exactly how Michael Collins met his death. Neither do I know who killed him. *Consequently I did not nor do not, by implication or otherwise, point the finger of suspicion or guilt at any individual anywhere in these pages*. I feel it necessary to emphasise this because of the attempts to unfairly sensationalise what I have written. I know that for a long number of years past extraordinary suspicions and rumours have been linked to the names of certain individuals, now dead, both on the Free State and Republican sides. I can only say that I have not found any solid evidence anywhere that would prove the truth of these rumours and suspicions.

I am afraid my critics will be most disappointed with this new edition. Instead of 'back-tracking' it does the opposite, and it takes many further steps in demolishing the hardened, crusted, entrenched prejudices of the past. It goes still further in showing that there are alternatives to the traditional account of Collins' death. I had to re-write large sections of the last two chapters in the light of all this new information which came my way. Here and there I have corrected some obvious errors and in a few places I have omitted matters which were suggested to me to be irrelevant and indeed in some doubt. But in general the theme that Collins could have met his death in any of at least three ways remains the same. It could also be said that this edition highlights more than ever *what an appalling national scandal it was that no inquest or inquiry was held into his death*.

I suppose I could truthfully say that this book began a long time ago, when as a young officer in the Irish army, I was serving in West Cork. As a university student I studied history and when I found myself stationed in this legendary corner of Ireland what could be more natural than to try and discover its most famous son, Michael Collins. I read all the biographies then available: Piaras Beaslai, Batt O'Connor, Frank O'Connor, Hayden Talbot, as well as many pamphlets and articles in newspapers. The nature of my military duties brought me into contact with some of Collins' closest friends. I also got to know many of the leaders who survived the War of Independence and the Civil War, as well as some of those who were involved in the ambush at Béalnabláth. These men talked freely about the stirring times of the past and in particular about Michael Collins. I visited both the place of his birth and the scene of his death many times and, although I am in no way psychic, I often felt that there was a living presence lingering around.

From these kaleidoscopic contacts there slowly emerged in my imagination a lively, dramatic and comprehensive picture of what seemed to me then to be the foremost Irish leader since Brian Boru.

Although nearly forty years have passed I have found no reason to change my mind. I saw that Michael Collins possessed to a high degree a unique mixture of all the outstanding qualities which stamped the great leaders of history. He had a clear, penetrating intelligence, a disciplined mind, an unerring grasp of the essentials of a situation. He was what one might call a realistic idealist. The ideals of many others around him, such as De Valera, Brugha, Lynch, were abstract and unrelated to reality. It seemed as if they loved the Republic more than the people who made up that Republic. But Collins was concerned with fact and he never allowed himself to get lost in a dense haze of words. His idealism was, therefore, all the greater because it was well grounded in the tangible. He signed the Treaty, not because of

9

what it represented, but because at the time, it was the surest road to the Republic.

Yet the tragedy here was, on the one hand the destructive attitude of his opponents, and on the other hand the fact that, unknown to him, a majority of the Provisional Government abandoned the Republic and accepted Dominion Status as a final solution. Their leader, W. T. Cosgrave, later made that quite clear: 'We intend,' he said, 'to become good members of the British Commonwealth.' Indeed by 1925 the Cosgrave Government had abandoned virtually everything for which Collins stood. They turned their backs on the idea of an eventual Republic and accepted our role as an integral part of the Empire. They agreed to a Northern State of six counties instead of three or at the most four counties as agreed between Collins and Lloyd George. They made an agreement which had already been rejected by Collins to hand over five million pounds per annum to Britain. The work of surrender was almost complete. Yet what a strange irony of fate in 1932 put De Valera into the role of Collins' successor as the dis-mantler of the Treaty. During his years of office he did almost all the things Collins forecast could be done, thus proving that at the time of the Treaty he was wrong and Collins was right.

Be that as it may, one thing seems sure: because of his insistence on the importance of the Irish language, and his acceptance of violence as a political weapon, Michael Collins would hardly qualify for membership of any political party in Dáil Éireann today.

Like all great men Collins was a very complex charac-ter. Behind his rough and rugged exterior there lay an unusually sensitive soul. He was capable of great magnanimity or merciless ruthlessness depending on the demands of the situation, yet that ruthlessness was rarely far from tenderness. He was deeply disturbed by the fact that he had to send so many men, even though they were enemies, to their deaths. But there was no other way and it was not the way he would have wished. Deep within himself there seems to have been an eternal struggle between the humanitarian and the soldier, between the saint and the killer. Again, like all the great captains he had his faults. Although he operated a first-class military intelligence system he had no political intelligence organisation whatever. It seems as if the British knew what was happening within the Irish cabinet but the Irish had not a clue as to what was happening in Westminster.

Sometimes his judgments of people could be very defective. His wholehearted acceptance of the ex-British army 'converts' to Republicanism may well, in the long run, have had ruinous consequences, not only for himself but for the Irish nation as a whole. The extent of these consequences we will know only when all the documents are made public. I do not suggest that Collins should have rejected these people — many of them may have been genuine enough — but he should have kept them far away from headquarters and far away from his own inner circle. Some ex-British soldiers, like Tom Barry, gave stalwart service on the battlefield and it is to such tasks that the abilities of these trained military men should have been directed.

Again, he failed many times because he trusted men smaller than himself who had little or no grasp of the complexities of a revolution and who could see things only in terms of black and white.

Even his greatest admirers would not claim that diplomacy was one of Collins' strong points. He did not wear kid gloves when in an angry mood. He abused Austin Stack frequently and openly for what he believed to be incompetence. It was Collins who brought Stack into the Cabinet and he was deeply disappointed at Stack's

11

performance. Once, Cosgrave fell asleep at a cabinet meeting and when he woke up Collins told him to go back to sleep again for all the value he was to the the meeting. He complained about Kevin O'Higgins to De Valera and accused O'Higgins of hiding in a monastery and neglecting his duties. Collins had very little hesitation in openly interfering in the affairs of his colleagues and this, coupled with his quick temper, sowed seeds that were later to yield a bitter fruit. Yet in spite of these failings he was complete master of the various and complicated tasks which he undertook to perform, many of which he had to undertake because they were neglected by others whose responsibility it was to deal with them. He was, effectively, running a revolution and he pursued that task relentlessly, irrespective of the feelings of others.

The rare and magnificent talents bestowed on him by his Creator he generously gave back to the Irish people. He became the one man who could have led us and welded us into a great nation. He had the greatness, the vision, the ability and, above all, the courage to bring this about, but a bullet at Béalnabláth put a stop to all his hopes and dreams, and dramatically changed the history of Ireland. It is with this mysterious bullet that the present book is concerned.

It has been a difficult, sometimes exasperating, book to write, but I have done my best to present as accurately as possible the welter of contradictory statements and reports about the death of Collins. While there is a lot of information concerning his life readily available, a kind of curtain of ambiguity surrounds his death. One is reminded here of Winston Churchill's famous saying: 'Truth is so precious that we must protect it with a bodyguard of lies.' The theory that Collins was killed by a ricochet was one of the great unnegotiated compromises of Irish history. It suited all

12

parties. It protected the IRA from the accusation that they deliberately shot our greatest hero. It protected the Free State from the accusation that, through neglect and carelessness, they allowed Collins to be killed. It was Emmet Dalton who first published the ambush details exactly a year after Collins' death when the Civil War was over. There were many who would regard this unexplained delay with some suspicion and say that as long as the Civil War lasted the Free State Government derived immense propaganda value from blaming his death on the IRA. With the ending of the Civil War it was felt that the IRA were finished for all time so there was little propaganda value to be derived from perpetuating the story further, and with mounting suspicion of Government negligence what more appropriate moment to launch the ricochet theory? No doubt this theory made a lot of people happy. They were all blameless and nobody was really responsible for the death of Michael Collins!

But compromises are never wholly satisfactory and there is usually a lingering suspicion that everything is not quite right. Down the years all kinds of such suspicions have been gaining momentum and today there is a substantial body of responsible opinion highly sceptical of this ricochet theory, which I now believe to be untenable, even though for many years I believed it to be the most likely explanation. It was only recently when I began to collect and evaluate the fresh evidence on the wounds that I realised what a nonsensical theory it was.

When I was writing this book I naturally met a few braggarts who usually said: 'Of course I know all about the death of Collins but my lips are sealed!' They generally knew nothing. But I met a far greater number of others who gave me invaluable help and who did everything possible to advise and assist me with information and with important leads. I would like to thank them all most sincerely.

Amongst those who helped me one deserves special mention, Mr Cormac Mac Carthaigh. For more than thirty years Cormac patiently and painstakingly researched the circumstances surrounding the death of Michael Collins and in the late sixties and early seventies he wrote a series of articles in the magazine *Agus* under the general title *Mícheál Ó Coileáin, Cé Dhein a Bháis a Phleanáil? (Michael Collins, Who Planned His Death?)* As I was at that time often out of the country I missed many of these articles and it was only within the last few years I had an opportunity to read the files in full. It was then I decided to write this book. Cormac gave me every help and encouragement and put at my disposal the valuable material he had accumulated in his long years of research. Were it not for this help, so generously given, I doubt if I could have written it, and here I would like publicly to express my deepest and sincerest thanks to him. *Go mba fada buan é!* Of course the use to which I put this information is my own and Cormac is in no way responsible for my opinions and conclusions. I would also like to say a special word of thanks to that wonderful woman Maire Comerford who made documents available to me that I might otherwise have found impossible to see.

Having finished the work I now freely admit I have only touched the tip of the iceberg. I know there is far more to be said but I could not say it because I failed to find sufficient proof to warrant its publication. For example, I was given good reason to suspect a close connection between the shooting of Sir Henry Wilson and the shooting of Michael Collins, but when I tried to investigate this line I found every door closed on me — indeed some banged in my face.

So this book then is no more than an opening of windows, a letting in of some fresh air to a very murky atmosphere, and I hope it may help to inspire those who have useful and informative documents in their possession to make them available. Michael Collins deserves better than that his memory should be left clouded in shabby mystery.

Finally, should any reader believe that there are errors of fact or interpretation in this book, I would be most grateful if they would be so kind as to write to me so that the matter could be considered for future editions.

J.M.F.
December 1981

1. The Life

The Irishman who thinks he can throw away his arms just as Grattan disbanded the Volunteers in 1789 will find to his sorrow that he has placed himself in the power of a cruel and relentless enemy.
— C. S. PARNELL

Michael Collins senior was sixty years of age when he wooed and wedded a young twenty year old girl, Mary Ann O'Brien. They had eight children in all and when old Michael was seventy-five years his last and youngest child, Michael, was born on 16 October 1890 at Wood-field, near Clonakilty. The family made a moderate living out of a ninety acre farm in this remote and isolated corner of West Cork. Later on they built a new dwelling house near a place known as Sam's Cross, so called in memory of a famous highwayman of the previous century, Sam Wallace.

The old man, like so many Irish peasants of the nineteenth century, was educated in an outlawed hedge-school where he acquired a good knowledge of Irish and French, and a working knowledge of Latin and Greek. This love of learning he was to pass on to his youngest boy. There are, no doubt, many pundits who would put forward the theory that growing up with a father in his late seventies could have a hindering, retarding effect on so young a child, but the opposite seems to have been the case in the Collins' household. Young Michael had a particularly close and friendly relationship with his father and seems to have gleaned from this relationship a wisdom beyond his years. Another side effect this close affinity had was to give the young boy a strong rapport with people much older than himself. In later life he was to say: 'Great age held something for me that was awesome. I was much fonder of old people in the darkness than of young people in the daylight.'

It is hard for us today, almost one hundred years later, to visualise what life was like then for a young boy growing up in Ireland. Poverty and a lack of the minimal comforts of life were the common heritage of the vast majority of the population. There was no electricity, no running water, no radios, no motor cars, no buses. For travel to the local towns there was only the ass and cart, the horse, or for the lucky few, a bicycle. A visit to far-away Cork or Dublin was something which happened only once or twice in a life-time and a person living near Rosscarbery would have little or no knowledge of the countryside around Bandon, Crookstown or Béalna-bláth. Food was of the simplest; stirabout, milk, potatoes, vegetables, eggs, coarse bread, and on the rare occasions when meat graced the table it was rabbit, fowl or home-cured bacon. But if there was grave material poverty the destitution of spirit had reached an all-time low. The power and the glory of the empire was at its height. To be an Irishman was to be virtually a slave with scant hope of ever getting further in life than the serving of English masters. The majority of the people had been so long servile that they had come to accept it as their natural state and had come to fear, honour and obey their oppressors. Like the sow in the dung heap they had come to love their own squalor. Victoria was on the throne and the fact that in the three terrible years after the Famine she permitted the eviction of two hundred and sixty thousand Irish men, women and children, most of whom died of starvation, did not prevent Irish lord-mayors, aldermen, arch-bishops, bishops and clergy grovelling and cringing before her on the few occasions she deigned to visit this country. Re-reading today the accounts of her visits to Dublin, Cork and Killarney it seems incredible to us that Irish public figures could ever have degraded them-

17

selves to the extent they did.

But this degradation was not entirely universal. Scattered here and there throughout the countryside there were more than a few rebels who refused to fawn; dissenters who kept their independence of mind; revolutionaries who preached and kept alive the spirit of nationalism and rebellion. The young Michael Collins was to come under the powerful and compelling influence of two such men.

The first of these was James Santry, a blacksmith whose grandfather had taken part in the 1798 Rebellion and whose father had forged pikes for the Risings of 1848 and 1867. The blacksmith's forge has always been one of the great assembly points of the Irish countryside, and is one of those places with a very special attraction for young boys who delight in blowing the bellows and tending the nervous horses for the busy smith. It was here that Collins heard from the lips of Santry stories of ancient Irish heroes, of Rebellions, of the Famine, of evictions and hangings, and above all of the local hero, O'Donovan Rossa, then still alive, whose savage treatment and torture in English jails had become part of the folk tradition of the West Cork countryside. Santry recounted how O'Donovan's jailers kept his hands frequently tied behind his back so that, thus handicapped, he had to use the toilet, and eat his meals off the floor in such a way that he was forced to lie on his stomach and lap like a dog. All these fiery tales of England's misdeeds and Ireland's wrongs must have had a profound effect on the impressionable mind of the young Collins, and almost certainly helped to shape the course of his future destiny.

The second great influence on his flowering mind was that of Denis Lyons, the local schoolmaster. Lyons was a member of the secret Irish Republican Brotherhood and he instilled his separatist ideals into the mind of his young pupil. Probably more important still, he guided Collins in his choice of reading and introduced him to the works of Charles Kickham, Michael Doheny, Canon Sheehan, O'Donovan Rossa and many other writers of a strong nationalistic turn of mind. Later Collins was to say of these two men: 'In Denis Lyons and James Santry I had my first tutors capable of — because of their personalities alone — infusing into me a pride in the Irish as a race. Other men may have helped me along the searching path to a political goal. . . nevertheless Denis Lyons and James Santry remain to me as my first stalwarts.'

In the years after the 1916 Rising it became fashionable to say that the writers of the Irish literary renaissance, such as Yeats, Lady Gregory and others were the inspiration behind the movement and that were it not for this influence there would have been no Rebellion or subsequent fight for freedom. This is somewhat of an exaggeration. Very few of those who fought in the 1916 Rebellion and in the years afterwards ever heard of Yeats, Lady Gregory or the Abbey Theatre. Certainly a few prominent leaders in the cities had, but the majority of the other leaders and fighting men did not even know of the existence of the Irish literary renaissance and could hardly name any of the writers associated with that movement. Men like Breen, Deasy, Mac Eoin and others were nurtured on an intensely nationalistic literature to be found in magazines like *Ireland's Own, Sinn Fein, The Shamrock, Irish Nationality* and books such as those Denis Lyons recommended to Collins. It was this literature, which circulated freely in Irish homes during the half-century preceding the Rising, this kind of literary curtain-raiser, which had a very profound effect upon many of those who participated in the 1916 Rising and the War of Independence.

As his mind matured the young Collins began to make

very perceptive and shrewd judgments on the Irish political scene. For example, he detested the Irish Parliamentary Party led by John Redmond and referred to them as 'slaves of England' and 'chains around Irish necks.' Although seemingly harsh, such sentiments were shared by many nationalists at the time. They felt that this party had let the people down by forgetting they were Irishmen and by becoming first and foremost loyal servants of the queen. On the other hand Collins developed a profound admiration for the movement inspired by Arthur Griffith, even though he could not have fully understood the deeper economic theories Griffith was trying to propound.

In his early 'teens Collins passed an examination for a clerkship in the post office and he was posted to far-away London where luckily enough his sister was also working. The transition to London from the romantic ruggedness of West Cork, with all its freedom and wild beauty, had somewhat of a traumatic effect on the young boy. Here he was at the very hub of the empire which had crushed and almost obliterated his country and his people, and as he strolled along through its magnificent streets, dotted with statues and memorials to renowned colonisers who built this dazzling empire on the 'blood, sweat and tears' of unfortunate natives, his sense of patriotism and love of Ireland became stronger, deeper, more intense and more determined. His years of exile and loneliness toughened and hardened his raw country nature and helped to form within him that great sense of realism which was to be such a predominant characteristic throughout his life. Here too, in this glittering city, he turned to things of the mind and began to read the great masterpieces of world literature, attend outstanding theatre performances, visit art galleries and concerts, all of which awakened his sensitive soul to other beauties and greatnesses which lay beyond his native Ireland. Like many other young exiles of the time he involved himself in the various Irish societies in London, such as the Gaelic League and the Gaelic Athletic Association, but his most significant step came when at eighteen years of age, following the example of his Cork schoolmaster, he joined the Irish Revolutionary Brotherhood, as it was called, a secret organisation dedicated to freeing Ireland by physical force. It later bacame known as the Irish Republican Brotherhood.

Earlier, as a result of British pressure, the IRB had been condemned by the Pope and the Irish hierarchy, but these condemnations were largely ignored, and it continued to flourish and attract new members. In the IRB Collins made his first contact with men like Joe O'Reilly and Sam Maguire, who were to be life-long comrades. Here his great flair for organisation began to show and rapid promotion within the brotherhood followed over the next two years.

About this time he also changed jobs, left the civil service and joined a reputable firm of stockbrokers, Horner and Company. His experience in the post office was, however, to stand him in good stead when he was organising his network of spies within the Irish postal service, as was his experience with Horner and Company when he later came to handling the finances of the proscribed Republic.

It was through the influence and teachings of the IRB that Collins came to realise a very fundamental truth: a truth to which Home Rulers and cultural Gaels had been blinding themselves for generations. That truth was: *The British yield only to physical force. Truth and justice, peacefully debated and discussed, they treat with scorn.* This truth, which must have been self-evident to anyone with even a moderate knowledge of the history of how Britain handles conquered peoples, was equally as true then as it was a hundred or two hundred years before. The majority of Irish politicians chose to ignore this simple fact, perhaps because it was inconvenient, or it might have had unpleasant consequences for their own personal ambitions; but the young Collins was far too great a realist to blind himself to it. The acceptance of this actuality was to dominate almost all his future actions, and to chart the course of his entire life.

Back in Dublin plans were well under way for the forthcoming Rebellion, so around Christmas 1915 Collins crossed over to meet the leaders and find out as much as he could of the plans that were being prepared. After extended meetings with the old veteran Tom Clarke and the young Sean Mac Diarmada he returned to London well briefed on what was likely to happen. It was the measure of how much they trusted him. He then made the important decision to give up his job and return at once to the Irish capital so that he could be on hand when the Insurrection broke out.

Through the influence of Joe McGrath he got a job in Dublin as secretary of the National Aid Association and later with the accountancy firm of Craig Gardiner and Company, and on 15 January 1916 he left England for good. The First World War was at its grim height and when giving notice he told his boss, with his tongue in his cheek, one presumes, that he was leaving to 'join the army'. He did not specify which army and the boss, believing there was only one army, warmly congratulated him and gave him a cheque for an extra month's salary. Crossing over on the boat he casually teamed up in the bar with a few British soldiers, and as they chatted and drank together he wondered silently within himself if he ever met them again would it be at the opposite ends of their rifles. In such ways is the web of human destiny woven.

Hardly any of the leaders of the 1916 Rising believed

that it would be a military success. Their greatest hope was that it might awaken the Irish nation from the pitiable mental slavery into which it had slipped; show the British occupying forces that Ireland would never be beaten; and perhaps inspire a physical force movement which would eventually liberate the country from its oppressors. And that is pretty much what happened. The men who signed the Proclamation of Independence knew that, in effect, they had signed their death warrants, but they believed it worthwhile. Militarily the Rising itself was a pitiful failure. Eight hundred untrained Irishmen held out for a week against five and a half thousand seasoned British troops and then, outnumbered and overpowered, surrendered. Collins fought in the GPO with the rank of captain, as ADC to Joseph Plunkett, but his relatively junior position gave him no real say in any major decisions. At one stage in the GPO he burst open two barrels of porter and emptied them down a drain. 'Too many Irishmen were drunk in 1798,' he said, 'that's not going to happen this time.'

Together with over two hundred other insurgents he was marched through the streets of Dublin en route to a prison ship for transportation to an English detention camp. On the way the Dublin people lined the streets, pouring abuse and vilification on the prisoners. The worst invective came from the 'separation' women, — the wives of the soldiers who were out on the European front and who were drawing what was known as 'separation' money — a great boon without the encumbrance of a drunken husband. They denounced the prisoners in the most obscene, foul-mouthed language, and broke ranks to spit in their faces. Outside the Rotunda hospital, where some of the prisoners were kept waiting, poor old Tom Clarke, who had already spent the best part of his life in British jails, was dragged

23

from the ranks, together with Willie Pearse and Edward Daly, stripped and publicly beaten by a Captain Lee Wilson Collins never forgot this savage, brutal scene and years later he located Wilson in Wexford and had him shot.

It was a desolate ending to a gallant fight. Once again England had won the battle, but this time she was to lose the war. A great miracle of stupidity took place. The British commander in Dublin, Sir John Maxwell, executed sixteen of the leaders and almost overnight the mass of Irish people, who were against the Rising, changed their minds and swung behind the insurgents. Their slavery was not so deep after all. The War of Independence began, and the vast majority of the population cast their lot, for better or worse, with the young men in their shabby trench-coats and outmoded weapons.

In the British prison camp the qualities of leadership which were part of his nature began to emerge and his fellow prisoners came to see the real Collins for the first time. He organised a highly successful campaign of non-co-operation with the prison authorities — refusal to do menial tasks, prison work, refusal to wear prison garb, refusal to answer roll-call — a campaign strangely similar to the recent H-Block protest:

'Sit down,' he said to his comrades. 'Refuse to budge. You have the British beaten. For a time they'll raise war. In the end they'll despair. Method, but unorthodox, has them beaten the whole time.'

The prisoners, including Collins, were transferred to Frongoch in Wales and the irony of the whole matter was that it could justly be claimed that this prison camp became the first Irish military school. Here the prisoners organised themselves into units and were given lectures on military tactics with particular reference to guerrilla warfare. Collins laid down the basis of his future influence through the close contact he made with prisoners from different parts of the country, who were deeply impressed by his forceful personality and organising ability. He also began to lay the basis of his intelligence system by finding out from each prisoner what friendly police or government officials he knew in his home district. With characteristic thoroughness Collins classified all this information for future use.

The action of the British in executing the leaders had its effect outside Ireland as well. In the United States, with such a large population of Irish extraction there were outcries and protests and many influential Irish organisations were bringing pressure to bear on the American Government to intervene on behalf of the hundreds of untried Irish prisoners in English jails, many of whom had nothing to do with the Rising. Britain, in the throes of the Great War, and with an eye on the possibility of the Americans entering on the allied side gave way, and released the unconvicted Irish prisoners on 22 December 1916.

Collins was now a free man, home in Ireland, no longer unknown, but with his reputation inside the movement greatly enhanced, and his star rapidly ascending. Even more important still, the prisoners who were incarcerated in Frongoch, beaten and demoralised, emerged as a highly organised guerrilla force who sensed that they had a crucial role to play in the future of the nation.

The Ireland these men returned to was not the same Ireland they left a few months before. They were now heroes and the whole political atmosphere had changed. The influence of the old Irish Parliamentary Party, which hitherto spoke for the Irish people and which condemned the 1916 Rising, was declining fast. There was a political vacuum which Collins recognised at once: 'Consider the situation,' he said. 'It is ripe for whatever one may wish. Both the British, and the Irish Parliamentary Party are in a corner driven there by what they have done and by the will of the people. There now exists a wilderness. . . Will any Irishman stand and wait and let this opportunity pass?' And, of course, the Irish did not stand by.

There was a by-election in North Roscommon, and the candidate put up against the Irish Parliamentary Party was a man whose son Sir John Maxwell had executed in 1916 and who had been expelled from the Royal Dublin Society for his nationalistic views, George Noble Count Plunkett. Collins was one of Plunkett's most tireless workers and is credited with the authorship of this masterly propaganda piece in Plunkett's election address:

> Because he will not associate with the Irishmen who cheered when his son was shot against a wall for loving Ireland, will you insult him in North Roscommon, as the Royal Dublin Society did and tell the British Government that he is not the man you want? No. There are Irishmen in North Roscommon yet.

Plunkett won by an overwhelming majority and refused to take his seat in the Westminster Parliament. This success was quickly followed by three others: Joseph McGuinness in Longford, who was still in jail and whose slogan was *Put him in to get him out,* W. T. Cosgrave in Kilkenny and a strange young teacher of mathematics, Eamon De Valera in Clare. Tim Healy, a pillar of the Irish Parliamentary Party was later to say when he lost his own seat: 'The Sein Feiners won in three years what we did not win in forty.' All of which seems to say that physical force has its points.

Now the two main strands in the Irish nationalistic movement, the IRB, advocates of physical force, and Sinn Fein who favoured political action, came together into one organisation which took the name Sinn Fein. The young mathematics teacher, Eamon De Valera, was elected President. De Valera had come into prominence as the last garrison commander in 1916 to surrender, and had subsequently impressed one section by what they thought to be his Republican single-mindedness and another section by what they believed to be his moderate outlook. It is said that when St Athanasius was composing his famous Creed he wanted to satisfy everybody so whatever he propounded in one sentence he contradicted in the next. The result was that his Creed was accepted by all the factors in the church as a work of profound wisdom. It seems De Valera took a leaf out of Athanasius' book. On his election as President he said: 'We do not wish to bind the people to any form of government.' Later on in the same speech he negated those sentiments when he said: 'It is necessary for us to be united now to the flag we are going to fight for, that of the Irish Republic. We have nailed the flag to the mast and we shall never lower it.' Here he scored a temporary success by uniting the militants and the moderates, but these double standards of his were to have devastating results later.

The military wing of Sinn Fein was the Irish Volunteers, later to become the Irish Republican Army, or better known as the IRA. De Valera was elected President, Cathal Brugha, a tough, uncompromising Republican was Chief-of-Staff and the young Michael Collins was appointed Director of Organisation.

We now enter perhaps the most important period of Collins' career. Sinn Fein had a resounding victory in the 1918 general election, winning seventy-five seats out of one hundred and five. The party refused to attend the parliament in Westminster and set up an Irish parliament in Dublin, known as Dáil Éireann, which formally proclaimed Ireland a Republic. De Valera was elected President, Arthur Griffith Vice-President and Minister for Home Affairs, Michael Collins Minister for Finance and Cathal Brugha Minister for Defence. As well as taking on this task, Collins also became Adjutant

General of the Volunteers, as well as Director of Intelligence. He was to become an outstanding success in all positions, but particularly as Director of Intelligence.

Many of those who worked closely with him and with whom I spoke agree that he tackled his various jobs with a degree of professionalism that was truly amazing in such a young man. As Director of Intelligence he studied the various Irish Revolutions of the past and correctly concluded that there was one basic underlying cause why they all failed: *the ranks of the revolutionaries were riddled with British spies*. It was, therefore, quite clear that the present volunteers hadn't a hope of winning a war against the British until he smashed their espionage system and built up an Irish intelligence organisation to the very highest standards. In this he was highly successful. He didn't win all the rounds as we shall see, but he won most of them and what was of vital importance he dealt the final knock-out blow which led the British to sue for peace. It is not true to say that Collins alone won the fight for freedom, but it is true to say that were there no Collins Ireland would have lost the war. He was the determinative individual responsible for the military defeat of the British in Ireland. Yet despite his great success here there was one serious defect in his organisation. He had no political secret service. He did not know what was happening in the inner circles of power in Westminster. This was a major flaw, particularly since there is strong evidence to suggest that the British had a fairly good idea of the thinking within the Dublin cabinet.

By 1919 the armed conflict was in full swing and it quickly became clear that it was Collins, and not his immediate superior Cathal Brugha whose responsibility it was as Minister for Defence, who was playing the major part in its direction. In the National Library in Dublin there are thousands of feet of micro-film of the confidential letters, directives and orders he issued to the volunteer leaders all over the country, many of these indeed quite sharp and critical. It was guerrilla warfare characterised by attacks on British convoys, ambushes and the capturing of police barracks. This latter deprived the British of a valuable source of intelligence since the police, who were the eyes and ears of Dublin Castle, were forced to live in the larger towns, thus leaving the countryside virtually in the hands of the IRA. He struck a severe blow also at British administration by ordering the burning of more than one hundred Income Tax Offices. This made quite a lot of people, who were not great patriots, happy as I'm sure it would in the present day.

Britain pursued the war with a ferocity and savagery that reached a new all-time low in human degradation— a savagery which at times went far beyond in barbarity the activities of the worst SS regiments in the Second World War. They recruited a paramilitary force, mostly criminals from English jails, who became known as the Black and Tans, and who were guilty of the murder, rape, torture and mutilation of innocent civilians; who burned out homes, destroyed villages and behaved themselves with a savagery in line with what had been going on for centuries. The inhuman treatment meted out by these Black and Tans shocked all right thinking people. In Cork city they cut the tongue out of one young prisoner, the heart out of another, the nose off another and battered to pieces the skull of a fourth. The bodies were so badly mutilated that their relatives could only identify them by their clothes. In the west of Ireland prisoners were tied together and had their legs roasted in a fire. In Meath a normal pastime of the Black and Tans was to tie prisoners behind their lorries, drag them for miles along the uneven roads and use them as target practice.

In recent years it became a trifle trendy amongst some politicians and amongst that new race of plastic men we have been spawning to try to whitewash over these deeds as if they never happened. It seems as if the old dormant slavery is asserting itself again. But facts are facts and, however unpleasant, must be accepted. This was England's traditional method of treating recalcitrant minorities who aspired to self-determination and it had a history of success behind it. 'The Irish are an inferior race,' said Bonar Law, 'and coercion is the only policy likely to succeed.' But this time they met their match in Collins, who was no wild tempestuous gunman, as they liked to think, but a disciplined, ruthless, highly efficient leader, the like of whom they had not met since they occupied the country seven hundred years before.

Deep in the very heart of British administration in Ireland, Dublin Castle, Collins had his spies. In all the important military centres throughout the country he succeeded in planting someone who kept him well supplied with information. One very human example of this was the case of an important British general who, after an exhaustive screening, chose the young widow of a British officer as his private secretary. Collins instructed his local intelligence officer to make up to the widow and pay court to her. This the officer did and ultimately won the lady over. Thereafter Collins got a copy of every confidential letter she typed. The matter had, however, a happy ending. When hostilities were over the couple got married. Collins organised his spies in post offices, sorting offices, buses, trains, ships, schools, whore houses and indeed everywhere a scrap of information could be had. One of his most important spies in Dublin Castle was the confidential typist, Miss Lily Mernin, who had access to secret files and provided Collins with the names of almost all the top British agents.

One very important part of his secret organisation was dockers and sailors. By this means he was able to import arms, gelignite and ammunition under the very noses of the customs officers and police. All this had a devasting effect on British military operations. Almost every move they made Collins knew of it and the IRA were waiting. In engagement after engagement they defeated the seasoned British army so that by mid-1920 the government in London were alarmed at the turn events had taken. They had won a World War, yet with 60,000 well armed and equipped troops they were unable to crush a small Irish guerrilla force of less than 3,000 and more humiliating still they knew that all this was due to one man, Michael Collins. 'The tenacity of the IRA is extraordinary,' said Tom Jones, Lloyd George's secretary. 'Where was Michael Collins during the Great War? He would have been worth a dozen brass hats.'

They now threw the entire British secret service, with its unlimited finance and personnel, into the fray. It was no longer a battle between two armies, but between two secret services as well; one with centuries of experience and unlimited resources behind it, the other untrained, with no resources, but with an unbreakable spirit. A sample of that spirit was the case of a young medical student, Kevin Barry, who endured unspeakable torture at the hands of British agents rather than betray his companions. In the midst of his agony his tormentors derided him with the fact that Collins and his leaders could not help him.

'What can they do for you now?' hissed his torturers. 'They can do nothing for me,' Barry answered, 'but I can die for them.' The following morning they hung him. When Collins was told about it he threw his head into his hands and burst into tears. 'The poor kid, the poor kid. . .' he kept sobbing.

The British now attempted to infiltrate the local IRA

battalions and brigades with spies who were, for the most part, Irishmen ready to sell their country for money. These spies were meant to be a back-up to a large number of wealthy landowners who passed on constant information. This policy, so successful in the past, did not work this time as they learned when the bodies of most of these informants were found shot on lonely country roads with placards around their necks containing the words: *Spies and Informers Beware.* In London the cabinet were getting desperate. They had calculated that it would now take 100,000 men to hold Ireland, and these men would have to be changed every six months, and the country was hardly worth it. Before seriously suing for a truce, however, they decided to have one last try. They believed that if they could get Collins, dead or alive, Irish military resistance would be broken and yet another Revolution suppressed. They picked sixteen of their best secret agents from all parts of the world, assembled them in Cairo, where they underwent a special briefing course on Michael Collins, his appearance, his habits, his haunts and eveything known about him. They then travelled singly to Dublin under false names and disguises posing as business executives with the sole object of getting Collins. It is said that a sum equivalent in our money to £200,000 was offered to whoever would kill or capture him. They worked independently of Dublin Castle, because it was felt Collins had too many contacts there, and they were a top security force. It is believed they were put under the command of a shadowy, chimerical, though able and ruthless figure, John Chartres, whom we will meet again. But Collins was all the time one step ahead. On the morning of 21 November, eight of his squads moved quietly in and shot fourteen of these spies in their lodgings and apartments. Of the two who cheated death that morning, one escaped, and the other, John

32

Chartres their reputed leader, could not be found anywhere. The reason given for this was that Chartres was in reality one of Collins' best spies and knew what was about to happen. But, like almost everything in the murky world of espionage, there is no real evidence to prove this.

The shooting of these top security men had a shattering effect on the morale of the English army in Ireland. They were shocked and stunned and could not believe that with all their mighty resources they could be so humiliated. The British Premier, Lloyd George frothed and fumed about 'murderers', 'rats' and 'gangsters', but while he was doing this in public he was secretly sending his first emissaries to Ireland to sue for peace. 'If I could see Michael Collins a settlement might be possible,' said Lloyd George. 'The question is whether the British people would be willing for us to negotiate with the head of a band of murderers.' But Lloyd George was not a man who allowed the swallowing of his words to choke him , and after many false starts, then some long hard bargaining, which lasted half a year, the Truce was signed on 11 July 1921 and the long war with England was over; Michael Collins was still free. The next major step was the signing of a Treaty between Ireland and England, and before dealing briefly with the part Collins played in that Treaty, it might not be out of place to have a look at a few of the principal characters involved.

First of all there was De Valera himself. He was President and head of the cabinet. He was a man of great ability in one sphere and very little in others. He was only a moderate administrator as he proved during the course of his subsequent career as chief of many Irish governments. He won election after election, not because of his endowments as a leader, but because of a singular lack of ability in any of his opponents. He had a strange streak of vain aloofness in his make-up and liked

33

to think of himself as a kind of Irish Lincoln; indeed he kept a statue of that great man on his office desk. But he fell far short of Lincoln as a statesman and saviour of his people. Yet there was one field in which he was absolutely supreme, and that was the field of negotiating and diplomacy. He had a subtle, adroit mind and a sharp, penetrating intellect. He could see the hidden hook in every proposal before it became evident to others. When Lloyd George told journalists that negotiating with De Valera was like trying to lift mercury with a fork, Dev innocently asked, 'Why does he not try a spoon?' He also possessed in a high degree that essential quality of all successful diplomats, the ability to make profound and seemingly far-reaching statements which were in essence meaningless. He was a Tallyrand to Collins' Napoleon. The more the war progressed the less confidence Collins had in De Valera and the less he trusted him. De Valera knew this: 'Collins did not accept my view of things. . .' he said, 'and was inclined to give public expression to his own opinions when they differed from mine.' Can one detect a hurt vanity here? While Collins believed in De Valera as a symbol he considered that as a Prime Minister he was incompetent and out of touch with reality.

When De Valera returned from his American tour in 1920, he wanted to ease off the war against the British and send Collins out of the country to America — exactly what the British would have loved. Those who believed that Childers was a spy say that it was he who suggested this idea to De Valera on instruction from Dublin Castle. But Collins nipped this incredibly stupid scheme in the bud: 'That long whore won't get rid of me so easily,' he commented to a friend.

Collins found it hard to tolerate that 'double standard' which was such a strong feature of De Valera's *modus operandi*. He could readily understand this type of political technique being used against the enemy, but why De Valera used it on his friends and supporters was something Collins was unable to comprehend or accept. Yet despite this Collins risked his life regularly to bring money to Mrs De Valera and her family in Greystones while Dev himself was in America.

Arthur Griffith might truly be called one of Ireland's greatest patriots. He was a brilliant journalist who could have commanded a top job on any newspaper, but instead he devoted almost his entire working life to writing for and editing small-circulation journals advocating Irish freedom. Even though he did not fight for Ireland in 1916, he certainly lived for Ireland afterwards. He was not a Republican. His favourite solution for Ireland was the 'dual-monarchy' of the Austria-Hungary empire, which he had carefully studied. But he willingly accepted Republicanism even though it failed to inspire him. The militarism of Collins frightened him, but Griffith respected him and defended much of what Collins did even though he did not agree with it. However it could not be said that they were close friends. Political freedom was of little attraction to Collins if Ireland was not Gaelic through and through, while on Griffith's side political freedom was of little use without economic freedom. He was essentially an economist rather than a politician and was far from content in the nebulous world of diplomacy. He could have been called the Sean Lemass or the Ludwig Erhard of the Revolution.

Cathal Brugha was the bravest of the brave. Although he was riddled with bullets in 1916, he still continued to be active in the struggle when another man would have called it a day. He was a diehard Republican, uncompromising and unyielding. For a long time he was obsessed with the drastic idea of shooting all members of the British cabinet as a solution to Ireland's problems. He had an extraordinary power over De Valera who has been accused of not standing up to him and of making many important decisions to please and placate Brugha rather than in the interest of the country. He would have excelled as a military leader fighting against desperate odds, but he was too inflexible to make good cabinet material.

His principal collaborator in the cabinet was Austin Stack, who shared most of his views including, at a later period, a dislike of and antagonism towards Michael Collins. Even De Valera admitted that Brugha was jealous of Collins, but Stack's antagonism had its origins in the fact that Collins reprimanded him many times for incompetence. Both Brugha and Stack would have served their country much better had they been given military commands instead of as members of the cabinet.

Erskine Childers was, and still is, a man of mystery and this mystery will only be cleared up when all the relevant documents have been released. Here I can only give the two sides of the story. A strong and influential body of opinion, which included Arthur Griffith and many of his colleagues, believed Childers to be nothing more than a British spy. Under pressure from Mary Spring-Rice he allowed his yacht *Asgard* to be used to ferry out-of-date arms to Ireland for use by the Volunteers in the fight against the British, and then proceeded to join the same British army almost immediately afterwards where he reached the rank of Major. He was a member of the British Intelligence Service and was seconded as Secretary to the abortive Irish Convention of 1917. He was subsequently supposed to be in charge of an important section of the British army responsible for all intelligence work west of Suez. It was said that his sole objective in involving himself in Irish affairs was to smash Sinn Fein and the Irish Volunteers.

But Childers himself had a different version. Speaking later at his trial he said: 'The collapse of the whole Convention and the attempt to force conscription convinced me that Home Rule was dead, and that a revolution, founded on the Rising of 1916, was inevitable and necessary, and I only waited till the end of the war, when I had faithfully fulfilled my contract with the British, to join the movement myself. With the formal establishment of the Republic in 1919, it became necessary for people like myself, of mixed birth, to choose our citizenship once and for all. I choose that of the Irish Republican Army.'

Gavan Duffy described Childers as 'one of the noblest men I've ever known.' But perhaps that which will endear him most to Irishmen is Winston Churchill's assessment: 'I have seen with satisfaction,' said Churchill, 'that the mischief making murderous renegade, Erskine Childers, has been captured. No one has done more harm. . . upon the common people of Ireland than this strange being activated by a deadly and malignant hatred for the land of his birth.' Many books and articles have been written about Childers, but the mystery remains. However, one thing is certain; he should never have been let into the higher echelons of power if there was even the slightest suspicion of his motives.

After a few meetings, an exchange of letters, all written in the Irish language accompanied by translations, and a barrage of telegrams between Lloyd George and De Valera, a formula was agreed as a basis for negotiation. This was done by De Valera without consulting the officers in the field. The first they learned of a truce was what they read in the newspapers. It was a grave error on De Valera's part. These men, who bore the brunt of the fighting while De Valera was safe and comfortable in America, whose victories had made the truce possible, felt treated as if they were insignificant nonentities. This unforgivable lack of communication between the politicians and the fighting men was one of the principal causes of the barbarous Civil War which was to follow later. Lloyd George issued the invitation '. . . to a conference in London on October 11th where we can meet your delegates as spokesmen of the people whom you represent with a view to ascertaining how the association of Ireland with the community of nations known as the British Empire may be best reconciled with Irish national aspirations.' This was a masterly piece of phraseology open to several different interpretations. However, one thing was absolutely clear from the meetings and correspondence between De Valera and Lloyd George and that was that *there was no question of a Republic*. Both the cabinet in Dublin and the Dáil understood that clearly. The importance of that fact cannot be over-stressed. Later there was a lot of talk about 'betraying the Republic' and 'fighting for the Republic', all of which was simply emotional nonsense. The Republic had been shelved before the negotiations even began and everyone concerned, particularly De Valera, knew that. The cabinet selected plenipotentiaries to go to London to negotiate with the British, but in effect it was De Valera who was the real selector. What kind of choice did he make?

Arthur Griffith was the leader. As we have seen he could not be called a Republican in any sense of the word and would be quite happy with dominion status. He was basically an economist with little experience of negotiating and even less will to negotiate. He was a sick man, exhausted and weary and he had no wish to go. He did all he could to get out of going and then reluctantly agreed. He said to De Valera: 'You are my chief and if you tell me to go I'll go. But I know and you know I can't bring back the Republic.' As well, he was drinking heavily and continued to do so increasingly during the negotiations.

Michael Collins was far more of a Republican than De Valera, but niceties of terms did not worry him too much and he would have no hesitation in taking oaths to the entire royal family once he could get self-determination and then use it to get a Republic. He pleaded almost on his bended knees not to be sent. There were many reasons for his reluctance, not the least the fact that he recognised he was totally unsuited to political negotiation. But one reason weighed particularly on his mind. He had grave doubts about De Valera. He believed he saw many straws in the wind which seemed to indicate that De Valera was blowing hot and cold with the Republic, and could not be fully trusted. Another reason why Collins did not want to go was because of a rumour current at the time about De Valera's last visit to Lloyd George to arrange the truce. According to the rumour Lloyd George brought De Valera into a room away from the others and told him bluntly that there could be no Republic because of the political effect on India and the other dominions. De Valera is supposed to have pleaded with Lloyd George and said: 'I am the President, the very embodiment of the Republic. How can I come over and negotiate a Treaty if I know in advance there can be no Republic?' The wily Welshman is said to have replied: 'You don't have to come. Send somebody else!' Collins seems to have heard this rumour which had the effect of making him distrust De Valera more. 'I was warned more times than I can recall about the *one,*' he said to a friend. 'And when I was caught for this delegation my immediate thought was how easily I had walked into the preparations.' Collins strongly suspected that the delegates, particularly himself, were only scapegoats, someone to put the blame on when it became nationally known that there would be no Republic. In the light of this rumour Lloyd George's report to the British cabinet in April, 1921 sounds curious: 'De Valera and Michael Collins have quarrelled,' he said. 'The latter will have a Republic and he carries a gun and makes it impossible to negotiate. De Valera cannot come here and say he is willing to give up Irish Independence, for if he did he might be shot.' This shows that the clear impression in Lloyd George's mind was that Collins, not De Valera, was the Republican.

Another delegate was Robert Barton, a County Wicklow landowner and cousin of Erskine Childers. Barton held a commission in the British army and was sent to Dublin in 1916 to assist in suppressing the Rising. He became a convert to Republicanism and was subsequently imprisoned many times by the British. The other two delegates were George Gavan-Duffy and Eamonn Duggan, possibly chosen because they were lawyers. The chief secretary to the delegation was Erskine Childers, detested by Griffith and, with the exception of Barton, not too well liked by the others.

Another important secretary was a gentleman we have met before, John Chartres, reputed head of the Cairo murder gang who were eliminated by Collins. This strange, shadowy, sphinx-like figure is more suited to a James Bond novel than to history. Who was he or what was he? As far as is known he was born in England and not in Cork, as some say. He was the son of a Major in the British army, and was educated in Germany and the University of London where he qualified in law. He joined the British army and rose to become an important officer in the intelligence group. Later he was put in charge of the intelligence department of *The Times*. He was, like Childers, another convert to Republicanism. 'Nineteen sixteen awakened me,' he told Sean T. O'Kelly, 'and from then on I regarded myself not as an Englishman but as an Irishman. All my love was now for Ireland. I would fight for her.' Sean T. evidently thought highly of him because during the period he spent in Paris trying to get Ireland recognised internationally he appointed Chartres' Italian wife as his personal secretary.

The British do not give an OBE lightly yet Chartres was offered one. The first question that springs to mind is what for? Strangely he refused this honour, but then it has been said that he was instructed to keep a low profile. Stranger still was the fact that having insulted the British crown by his refusal he was appointed in 1919 to head the important British Department of Labour in Dublin. He came over to Dublin to live and frequented all the best hotels and clubs immaculately dressed and sporting a monocle. He had known Collins for about a year and when he changed residence to Ireland he renewed his acquaintanceship. I do not think there can be much doubt about the fact that he was in reality a British intelligence agent. But was he a double agent working for Collins? The paid informer is rarely satisfied with deceiving one side. He has an irresistible urge to work both ways. Collins and himself were frequently in each others' company and once when Chartres disappeared for a while Collins told his friends: 'John is not feeling so well. He is gone to Egypt to get a little sun and rest.' Why not the Canary Islands or the Riviera? Why Egypt? Could it be that he was present at the briefing of British intelligence officers in Cairo? Could he have been the expert lecturing them on Collins? After Bloody Sunday when all the Cairo agents were shot, Chartres resigned from this job in the British civil service and came over full-time to the Irish cause. De Valera evidently trusted him for he appointed him as Chief Executive of the Irish White Cross, an organisation to help the dependants of Irish Republican soldiers, and later as an emissary to Berlin. And next he turns up as Secretary and Adviser to the Irish delegation negotiating the Treaty. How come? The only clue we have is that when Austin Stack was pressing to have a good constitutional lawyer travel with the delegation, Collins assured him: 'We have John Chartres acting for us.' That in fact was not an accurate answer to Stack's question. Chartres was a specialist in Workmen's Compensation Law and knew little or nothing about Constitutional Law. He seems to have spent the period of the Civil War as a trade representative of the Provisional Government in Berlin and afterwards he was given a job in the Department of Industry in Dublin. He lived in Rathgar and died in May 1927 at the age of forty-five.

This then was the team sent over to London to negotiate a treaty with a British delegation. Griffith, Collins, Barton, Gavan-Duffy and Duggan, with four secretaries, Fionan Lynch, Diarmuid O'Hegarty, Childers and Chartres and another ex-British officer, Emmet Dalton as military adviser. The selection of Dalton for this responsible position is very hard to understand. His participation in the war against the British was negligible and he had virtually no experience of what was happening outside Dublin. It is strange that someone like Deasy, Lynch, Robinson, Kilroy or Aiken who had proved themselves competent military leaders, and who had a wide and detailed knowledge of the state of the army, was not chosen. The powerful British delegation was led by the Prime Minister himself, Lloyd George, and comprised of Sir Austin Chamberlain. Lord Birkenhead, Sir Hamar Greenwood, Sir Laming Worthington-Evans, Winston Churchill and Sir Gordon Hewart.

Looking at the Irish delegation it is no exaggeration to say that they were simply no match for the British and should never have been chosen. They were disunited, some Republicans, some not, and because of the quibbling, hair-splitting, and in-fighting in the Dublin cabinet, they had no clear idea of what they wanted or how far they could go. On the other hand the British were united and of one mind. They were going to give Ireland a measure of freedom within the framework of the empire and no more. The majority of the Irish delegation did not want to go because they realised that they did not have either enough experience or the necessary qualifications for such a delicate and important job. All the British delegation were quite pleased and honoured to act and they had no doubts about their qualifications to deal with the Irish.

One unusual facet was that with the Irish delegation there were two ex-British army officers and two ex-British intelligence agents, who may or may not have still been active on the British side. Worse still, hovering in the background, keeping a low profile, was one of the most unprincipled and deceitful of Irishmen, Tim Healy, friend of Lord Beaverbrook and Lloyd George. How Collins and Griffth could have regularly sought advice and counsel from this individual, throughout the negotiations, is simply beyond comprehension.

Needless to say there were no ex-IRA officers on the British team! However one looks at it, the odds were heavily stacked against the Irish. It was like David and Goliath, except that David had no sling and the Dublin cabinet made sure his hands were tied behind his back.

Was there an alternative? I think there was. De Valera himself was an expert negotiator with all the qualifications and abilities necessary to deal with the British. He proved his worth in his initial discussions with Lloyd George who had a very healthy respect for him and realised quite well that he could not pull the wool over his eyes. De Valera should have gone himself and faced his opposite number. The excuse that he wanted to act as a brake on the delegation is just not credible. When De Valera compared himself to the captain of a ship, Collins quipped: 'Yes. A captain who sent out his crew to sea and tried to direct operations from the land.' Instead of an unwieldy confused delegation which the British quickly split up and exploited, he could have brought not more than two with him, two moderate Republicans such as, say, Count Plunkett and Prof. Daniel Corkery; shrewd, tough, astute men who would not panic or be stampeded, whose discernment and hard-headedness would have been more than a match for their opponents. With such a triumvirate the odds would have been considerably reduced, and the ultimate Treaty could have been, at worst, ideologically better, but enough to prevent the Civil War. Why did he not take such a course of action? His enemies would say that he wanted to go down in history as the Republican visionary, the incorruptible Irishman, the man who symbolised all the aspirations and hopes of seven hundred years, and that he knew perfectly well there was no hope of a Republic; that he did not want to be associated with anything else and so threw Griffith, Collins and the others to the wolves and let them appear as traitors and turncoats.

I think, however, there could be a more charitable explanation. In the field of diplomacy I believe De Valera was world class. I feel he could stand side by side with the greatest diplomats of history and out-manoeuvre any of them. This was his special forte and in subsequent years he proved this over and over again. His handling, for example, of our neutrality in the Second World War was little short of miraculous. I do not think that thousands of men of my generation should ever forget that our bones would be whitening the beaches of Omaha or Dunkirk were it not for the fact that De Valera's diplomatic brilliance saved us from this fate.

In other matters, however, he fell far below the necessary minimum for good leadership. He had a certain political cuteness which impressed the masses, but in the handling of men and affairs at close range he was a bungler and he badly bungled the Treaty negotiations. It was as if the managing director of a large construction company engaged in the building of a huge viaduct, sent out his accountants to do the job and kept his engineers at home. I think De Valera will have to be held account-able to history for this colossal blunder which had such irretrievable and irreparable consequences.

The plenipotentiaries negotiated for two months. They were divided, outwitted and out-manoeuvred. They finally came to Dublin early in December 1921 with a draft Treaty and could get no clear instructions from the cabinet. 'I've been there all day,' complained Collins to Tom Cullen, 'and I can't get them to say Yes or No, whether we should sign or not. . . I don't know whether we're being instructed or confused.'

They went back to London and a few days later signed the Treaty giving Ireland dominion status, but with an oath of allegiance and partition. They were absolutely entitled to do this since they were given power by the Dáil to 'negotiate and conclude' a Treaty. When some Dáil deputy objected to these powers, De Valera threatened to resign if the plenipotentiaries were not given them.

'I've signed my death warrant,' sighed Collins. De Valera immediately repudiated the Treaty, but the Dáil accepted it. In a general election the people accepted it too. But the anti-treatyites felt the public had no right to do wrong and they militarily occupied the Four Courts and other buildings throughout the city and country. The British government gave an ultimatum to Collins and Griffith which in effect said: 'You put a stop to this at once or if you don't we will come in and do so.'

Collins and Griffith acted. They put Emmet Dalton in charge of the operation under the direction of Tom

Ennis. Dalton surrounded the Four Courts with the new Free State Army. He did not accept Collins' advice to cut off food and water and thus force the occupants to surrender. Instead, he borrowed artillery from the British and shelled the building. The Civil War had begun.

It was to be a most savage, hateful and cruel war which cost the country the lives of virtually all its outstanding leaders. It is still not clear how it started. According to the Republicans they were loading their arms onto lorries and would have evacuated the Four Courts by 8 a.m. in the morning. Had the shelling not started at 4 a.m., they say, there would have been no Civil War. There clearly seems to be a need for a definitive study on the actual commencement of hostilities.

2. Accident of War?

Nothing hurts a new truth more
than an old error — GOETHE

Throughout the country units of the anti-Treaty forces remained in possession of various barracks in cities and towns in defiance of the Provisional Government which was set up under the terms of the Treaty and which was presided over by Michael Collins, because there was an agreement that Arthur Griffith would remain President of the Republic until the formal coming-into-being of the new state. These units constituted themselves as the Irish Republican Army and openly proclaimed that they were fighting to re-establish the Republic which those who signed the Treaty had betrayed.

This, of course, was an illusion. De Valera himself had dropped the Republic long before the Treaty negotiations had started, so that in effect what these men were really fighting for was Document No. Two, De Valera's hair-splitting alternative to the Treaty, even though the rank-and-file believed they were fighting for a Republic. History forever seems to repeat itself. At the Battle of Aughrim fifteen thousand Irish soldiers died in the belief that they were fighting for the freedom of Ireland, the Republic of its day, when in reality they gave their lives in an effort to put James II on the throne in London. In the First World War thousands of Irishmen died for what they believed to be the freedom of small nations, when in reality they gave their lives to consolidate an empire which was a past master at crushing and subjecting small nations. In the Second World War millions of allied soldiers died believing that they fought to free Poland and other European countries from a tyrant, when in reality they gave their lives so that another tyrant, reputed to have twenty-five million murders to his credit, might subject half of Europe to slavery. The politicians always seem to win and the soldiers never seem to learn. It was so in Ireland in 1922. In a recent book, *Michael Collins and the Treaty* by T. Ryle Dwyer, it comes across quite clearly that De Valera's rejection of the Treaty had little to do with Republican principles and had a lot to do with his struggle for power over Collins.

De Valera tried to resurrect the old Dáil Éireann which had declared itself Republican, but this failed because it was only a fantasy and had no existence outside his own mind. The Republican forces were then responsible to no elected body. Liam Lynch who was their supreme commander was an undoubted patriot but had a completely unrealistic and over-optimistic view of the chances of success. De Valera joined as a private and was later made captain. Yet despite the fact that many of the leaders of the IRA, particularly Liam Lynch, treated him in an off-hand way as if he were unimportant, he was still a powerful rallying point for all anti-Treaty opinion.

The IRA had little chance of a military success. They were poorly armed and heavily outnumbered by a Free State army with a strong backbone of well-trained ex-British soldiers who joined up after their demobilisation and were well-equipped with all the arms and armament they required. They had, too, the backing of the populace and the authority of an elected government behind them.

The fighting in Dublin began in late June 1922 and in a matter of ten days or so it had ended in a complete victory for the Free State troops there. Among the casualties on the Republican side was that sterling and ardent patriot Cathal Brugha. Rather than surrender he rushed out of the blazing Hamman Building firing his two revolvers and was mortally cut down by machine-gun fire. After Brugha's death Collins wrote to a friend: 'Many would not have forgiven — had they been in my place — Cathal Brugha's attack on me on January 7th. Yet I would forgive him anything. Because of his sincerity I would forgive him anything. At worst he was a fanatic — though in what has been a noble cause. At best I number him among the very few who have given their all that this country — now torn by Civil War — should have its freedom. When many of us are forgotten, Cathal Brugha will be remembered.'

The story of defeat was much the same all over the country. The IRA lost ground heavily and by August most of the cities and towns were in Free State hands. Then on 12 August the young state suffered a shattering blow. Arthur Griffith, sick, tired and heartbroken, burst a blood vessel and dropped dead. Collins was now the man responsible for bringing the war to an end. He returned from Limerick, where he was on inspection, for Griffith's funeral. At the graveside Dr Fogarty, Bishop of Killaloe, said to him: 'Michael, you should be prepared — you may be the next.' 'I know,' answered Collins quietly. A day later he wrote to a friend: 'There seems to be a malignant fate dogging the fortunes of Ireland; for at every critical period in her story the man whom the country trusts and follows is taken from her. It was so with Thomas Davis and Parnell and now with Arthur Griffith.' His own rendezvous with fate was just round the corner. His day of destiny was 22 August. He was to have married his girlfriend, Kitty Kiernan, that day, but the wedding was postponed. Had he a premonition of his death? 'I'll make no girl a wife just to make her a widow?' he said to a friend. 'The wedding will keep for a few weeks; in that time I'll end this business if it does not end me first.'

Collins decided to resume his inspection of the south, which had recently fallen to Free State troops, and on 20 August he left Dublin early in the morning with an escort said to have consisted of three officers and twelve men. They travelled via Roscrea, where they breakfasted, on to Limerick where after a short inspection they had lunch and where it seems some of the escort were changed, thence to Mallow and finally reached Cork around nine or ten o'clock that evening. When they arrived at the Imperial Hotel which was the headquarters of General Emmet Dalton, a close friend of Collins, and commander of the Free State troops in the south, Collins found the two sentries asleep. He lifted them up, one in each hand, banged their heads together and continued on through the hall.

On Monday, 21 August, Collins carried out a number of inspections in and around Cork city. In the light of subsequent events an incident which took place during one of these inspections assumes considerable importance. As the Collins' party was leaving Ballincollig Barracks they noticed some of the sentries manhandling a civilian motor-cyclist. When Collins intervened and asked what was wrong he was told that the motor-cyclist was trying to see him. Collins then asked this civilian what he wanted. The civilian replied: 'I'm from Liam Lynch. I would like to speak to you.' Both men then moved some distance away from the rest of the company and after about ten minutes conversation the motor-cyclist left. What was discussed at the brief meeting is unfortunately unknown.

After the inspection, the convoy drove to Macroom where Collins inspected the garrison and had a meeting with Florence O'Donoghue, a neutral officer, highly respected by both the IRA and the Free Staters. Again what transpired at this meeting has not been made public. However, it seems to have been an important meeting and Collins gave O'Donoghue a safe-conduct pass. Its importance lies in the fact that it had a bearing on Collins' whole outlook at this time on the Civil War. There is now no doubt but that he was trying to bring hostilities to an end and he hoped to reach some face-saving agreement with the leaders on the other side. It is known that he had arranged to meet secretly with some high ranking neutral officers in Cork the following evening to try and get negotiations started. It is also known that some of his cabinet colleagues, who had now finally settled for membership of the British Commonwealth and who had abandoned the Republic, were strongly opposed to his moves and regarded him with suspicion as trying to run with the hare and hunt with the hounds. Their feeling was that they were winning the Civil War and that they should continue without negotiation until the IRA were brought to their knees and surrendered unconditionally.

By a strange coincidence Liam Deasy, the officer commanding the First Southern Division IRA and by far the ablest military leader produced by the revolution, had called a meeting of senior IRA officers for 22 August at Béalnabláth, about twenty miles from Cork. The meeting was called to discuss future strategy after the heavy defeats suffered in Cork, Kilmallock and Limerick and also on the agenda was the question of ending the Civil War. Since most of these officers were on the run and their time of arrival could not be forecast, the meeting was scheduled for a date rather than for a precise hour. If all the officers were present the meeting would have started on the morning of 22 August, but as many of them had still not arrived the meeting was postponed until eight o'clock that evening.

Another visitor who had come into the area the day before was Eamon De Valera. He was now doing all in his power to bring the Civil War to an end and had just left the IRA Chief-of-Staff, Liam Lynch, in the Fermoy area. Lynch was not anxious to end hostilities except on his own terms and not only did he give De Valera the brush-off, but he sent a dispatch to Deasy asking him not to give any encouragement to De Valera. Deasy and De Valera discussed the ending of the Civil War far into the night at Sullivans of Gurranereagh. Deasy was favourable to De Valera's point of view and despite Lynch's request, he promised De Valera to have the whole matter discussed that evening at the officers' meeting.

So here we have Collins, on the one hand, coming to Cork to try and end hostilities, and De Valera coming to the same place for the same purpose. One cannot help posing the question: Was it really a coincidence? It has been said that they had arranged to meet at Béalnabláth but I can find no evidence of this. It has also been said that the shots fired by the ambush party that evening were merely to inform the officers at Béalnabláth that Collins was coming, and that the Collins party mistook them for an attack, jumped out and returned fire, and so the ambush began. Again I can find no evidence to support this theory.

On Tuesday, 22 August Collins left Cork around 6.15 in the morning with a convoy which consisted of a motor-cycle scout, Lieutenant Smith, an open Crossley tender with two officers, two Lewis-gunners, eight men armed with rifles, a touring car with Collins, Emmet Dalton and two drivers, Corry and Quinn, and finally an armoured car with revolving turret and Vickers machine-gun. A normal crew of four manned this armoured car.

Now we come to the first of many tantalising questions which will crop up regularly in this book. *Who selected this escort for Collins?* Some of these men were ex-British army personnel, who knew virtually nothing of the West Cork countryside. His driver, Corry, for example, was from Cheshire and spoke with an English accent. Jack Swan was Collins' regular driver in Dublin. The night before the convoy left for Cork he was told he would not be driving Collins. Why was his usual bodyguard of men, such as Tobin, Cullen and others, not with him? Although it can be presumed that most of the convoy were loyal to Collins, yet to entrust the life of a Commander-in-Chief to any escort other than one which was a hundred-per-cent screened could be asking for trouble. Here one must point the finger of criticism at Dalton who accompanied Collins and who was responsible for his safety in the south. Before leaving the city Dalton should have provided a bodyguard of Irishmen who knew the West Cork countryside and who had experience of rural, guerrilla warfare. He had enough such men under his command in Cork. He should also have thoroughly screened every individual member of that escort.

The convoy set out for Bandon, Clonakilty, Skibbereen via Macroom. *Why via Macroom?* This would put an extra twenty miles on them, through a countryside where they could expect roads blocked and bridges blown. He was in Macroom the evening before and carried out his inspection. Why should he want to go there again the following morning? Had O'Donoghue contacted IRA officers who were in hiding at Ballyvourney, near Macroom and had he a message for Collins about the proposed meeting in Cork? There must have been some good reason for that round-about trip to Macroom.

They left Macroom about 8 a.m. and brought a guide with them to show them the way to Bandon. When they reached the village of Béalnabláth they stopped to ask for the right road. It was a strange twist of fate that the young man who gave them directions was an IRA sentry who had just hidden his rifle in a bush while taking a short rest. He gave them specific directions but was sharp enough to recognise Collins which fact he later reported to his superiors. Here we must ask: *Why was it necessary to enquire the way from a stranger? Why were the maps not consulted?* It is a fact that they had maps with them. The last photograph taken of Collins just before they left Bandon that evening shows Dalton sitting beside him reading a map. It is a basic principle of military movement that maps are always used. A military convoy travelling through hostile territory does not stop casually and ask the way as if they were tourists. If it is absolutely necessary to seek directions then the person from whom such directions are sought must be arrested and brought with the convoy so that he cannot inform anyone as to its destination. The neglect of this simple military principle here was a primary cause of the death of Collins, but no officer was ever court-martialled or punished for this appalling military blunder. Here again one must fault Dalton. He was a trained, experienced officer and he should never have been a party to, or even allowed, such a grave military error.

About half-an-hour after the convoy left Béalnabláth, Liam Deasy arrived with De Valera in a pony and trap. Here they found out about the convoy and about Collins' presence. Tom Hales, the IRA Brigade Commander, had decided to lay an ambush in case the convoy returned by the same route. When De Valera heard this he said that it would be a great pity if Collins were killed because he would be succeeded by lesser and meaner men. In view of that perceptive and important statement it is extraordinary that he did not use his influence to scotch the whole idea of an ambush. If he had done so it seems reasonable to assume he would be listened to. Deasy then handed De Valera over to a guide who brought him safely to north Cork. Deasy returned to

Gurranereagh where he had a lot of administrative matters to attend to in preparation for the meeting.

The ambush party was composed of approximately twenty or twenty-two men in all. About half of these were not officers, but ordinary volunteers who were mostly members of local companies and who were there as a kind of protective force to ensure the safety of their leaders attending the meeting. When the meeting had been postponed Hales thought it advisable to occupy all present in some useful work, just in case they might be tempted by the public house on this hot August day, and so he marched the lot about half a mile along the Bandon road where they took up an ambush position. This was good sound thinking on Hales' part, yet it is tempting to speculate that if all the officers had turned up on time and the meeting started there might have been no ambush.

Meanwhile the convoy drove to Bandon where Collins spent a long time in private conversation with the Free State commander there, Major General Sean Hales. The Hales family were particularly close to Collins and all brothers played a leading role in the War of Independence. Donal Hales, who was a language teacher living in Genoa, was the Collins agent in Italy and he was especially successful in countering the false information being put about by the British agent, Gerald O'Donovan, ex-priest, novelist, and Corkman from near Bandon. It was particularly sad, but by no means unusual at the time that this wonderful family should be divided by Civil War. Tom Hales, who had fought the Black and Tans so bravely, now took the opposite side to his brother Sean and was a Brigade Commander with the IRA. 'I would prefer to have one Tom Hales with me than twelve other men,' remarked Collins. It was all the more poignant that as he spoke these words Tom Hales was preparing the ambush at Béalnabláth.

There seems to be little doubt now, but that the topic of conversation between Collins and General Sean Hales was the ending of the Civil War and, in particular the meeting being arranged with neutrals to take place in Cork that evening. It is also significant that immediately after his session with Collins, Hales left for Cork, and it subsequently became known that he was one of those involved in setting up this important meeting.

The convoy now left for Clonakilty where they lunched and moved on to Skibbereen via Rosscarbery. Nearby Collins met his brother Seán and some relatives. He said to Sean: 'Tonight I must get back to Cork. I will not leave Cork until the fighting is finished.' The convoy had drinks in White's pub and it seems as if Collins absented himself for half-an-hour or so. One version says that he wanted to talk privately with his relations, another version says that he had a conference with local IRA leaders about bringing the war to an end.

At Rosscarbery a rather strange thing happened. The officer in command of the Free State troops there, Captain Seán McCarthy, told Collins that there were a number of ex-British army soldiers in his unit and he had reason to believe that they planned to shoot him (Collins). He had, however, no proof, but as a precaution he took their rifles from them and confined them to barracks. He warned Collins to be careful as some of the ex-British army men were not to be trusted. Collins listened to all this in silence and made no comment on it. As he was leaving Rosscarbery he shook hands with McCarthy and said: 'I'm going to put an end to this bloody war as quickly as possible.'

The convoy then proceeded on to Skibbereen where he inspected the garrison and had discussions with the officers in charge. It was here he had an interview with that doughty old amazon, the novelist, Edith Somerville. She flounced in and demanded that he keep the 'murderers and ruffians' away from her sheltered little corner of the empire in Castletownsend. It was also about this time too that she wrote: 'The scum and the dregs of this wretched country are now in power. I don't know where my dear old Ireland has gone.'

The convoy left Skibbereen about 5 p.m. and drove back through Clonakilty as far as Bandon, where they met some of the Free State officers and had tea. From Bandon the party set out for Cork via Macroom. Once again the question must be asked: *Why via Macroom?* The normal and shorter road to Cork is through Innishannon and even though a bridge on that road was blown earlier it had been repaired. It was this route that Sean Hales and his convoy took earlier in the day and it was quite passable. What was in Macroom and why did Collins want to go such a long distance out of his way to visit this town and for *the third time in twenty-four hours?* And why did he return through Béalnabláth, which was militarily one of the most dangerous roads in the whole county? In his memoirs of the Civil War, *Brother Against Brother,* Liam Deasy finds it extraordinary that the convoy took this route back since there were three or four other more direct routes to Cork which were free of obstructions.

Meanwhile back at Béalnabláth as evening closed in the ambush party came to the conclusion that the convoy was not going to return by this route and so they decided to withdraw; the officers to hold their meeting and the covering party to go home. Consequently the main body moved away in the direction of Newcestown and began to separate and disperse. Tom Hales and a number of officers walked back towards Béalnabláth where they met Liam Deasy and Tom Crofts and all adjourned to the public house for some food and drinks. They did, however, leave behind five armed men to clear away an old cart which they had dragged across the road as a block, and to remove a mine. Two of these men came down towards where the cart was and three remained on the high parallel laneway as a look-out and protection. One of the men disconnected the mine and the other was dismantling the cart, which was around a bend and not visible to any approaching convoy, when the men on the hill saw the motor-bike, the tender, and the rest of the cars, and as much in warning as anything else, opened fire. The convoy stopped and the fighting began. It was around 8 p.m. GMT. There is no satisfactory answer as to why Lieutenant Smith and the tender had to stop at all, if, as has been said, the cart across the road had been pushed sufficiently to one side, and there was room enough for the tender and other vehicles to squeeze around it. *(See Sketch Map, Appendix A)*

Here we have another instance of grave military misjudgment. There is a normal tactical procedure put into effect when a moving convoy comes under fire and this is something that not only every officer, but every corporal, should know. This procedure aims at out-flanking the attackers. In this instance the armoured car could have backed a few hundred yards and moved up a laneway on the Bandon side. This action would have put the attackers to flight at once. Alternatively the armoured car and/or Lewis gunners could have given covering fire while a section tried to outflank the attackers on the Béalnabláth side. It seems as if a section did try to do this but failed to follow through to where the last two IRA men were. Collins and Dalton should *not* have taken part in the fight. They should have remained under cover of the touring car, the tender, or indeed got into the armoured car. There they could have waited for twenty minutes until darkness fell. It was the height of foolhardiness for two general officers to expose themselves to the risk of death while there were adequate combat soldiers available. Collins may be excused in that he had no military training, but Dalton should have known what to do and should have put his foot down however impulsive Collins may have been.

There are in all four published eye-witness accounts from the Free State side of what happened and each account differs from the other on a number of significant points. This is understandable as it is generally recognised that different people see things in a different way and consequently make mistakes. I give these accounts here with my own comments in italics.

The first to be published was that of the motor-cyclist, Lieutenant Smith. His account was not written by himself, but given in the form of an interview to newspaper reporters and published two days after the ambush in the daily and evening papers. In these circumstances it should be regarded with caution.

When the party arrived at the scene of the ambush, fire was opened on them. 'I immediately put on full speed,' said Smith, 'and rode right through for about 300 yards. *(This is wrong. If he rode that distance he would have gone beyond the scene of the ambush. He probably rode on 50 yards.)* One bullet struck the handlebar of my motor-cycle and injured my left hand. I saw a large cart with a wheel off drawn across the road in the form of a barricade, and I dismounted and ran into the ditch for cover. The cart completely filled the road which is narrow at that point. *(This has been disputed.)* After a minute or two I crawled along taking advantage of the little cover which the ditch afforded to see how the others fared. A few seconds elapsed and then the Crossley tender came up and stopped first where I was. I shouted to them to get under cover and under the direction of Commandant O'Connell the men dismounted and divided into two parties. Heavy firing was, of course, going on all this time, and our party had not yet commenced to reply. *(This is hard to credit. The range was only about 130 yards and surely someone would have been hit.)* My motor-cycle and the tender were left on the road. One party then immediately opened fire on the attackers at both sides of the road with a Lewis gun and rifles. *(This statement is rather mysterious. The attackers were only on one side of the road.)* Notwithstanding the heavy fire being directed on us the other party ran to the cart across the road, and attacking the barricade vigorously moved it aside, thus leaving the road open. This work occupied a very considerable time, during which we kept up a continued fire on the attacking party. Meantime the Leyland touring car and the armoured car had stopped some distance further up the hill *(there is no hill — only a very gentle slope)* and we could hear the fight going on at this end also. The attackers were spread out along the slopes at both sides of the road for fully a quarter of a mile. *(Presumably he means the laneway not the road. The impression that there was a large body of attackers is wrong. Smith is inclined to exaggerate numbers and distances. In another newspaper he was attributed with saying that there were 200 attackers.)* The Leyland car was stopped by direction of the Commander-in-Chief, who with Major General Dalton and the two drivers took cover behind the fence about a foot high. *(How did Smith know that Collins ordered the car to be stopped? Obviously he discussed the matter with someone before making the statement.)* This, however, left them exposed to the fire of the party on the other side of the road. *(Again mysterious. Perhaps he means the lane running west.)* The armoured car was in action a little further up. At the lower end of the road we kept firing and after some time drove back the ambushers on the right hand side of the road. *(Lane?)* They seemed to retreat over the top of the hill and the firing from this direction practically ceased. I went up around the brow of the hill after a little while in order to reconnoitre and as far as I could see this section of the irregulars had gone back over the hill. This gave us the opportunity to open a more intensified fire on the attackers on the other side, who were concealed around the farmhouse and amongst the shrubbery and bushes across the stream. *(There is no farmhouse across the stream.)* We picked off a couple of them and could see them fall. Another was crossing a gap and was hit. *(There were no IRA casualties.)* Our party continued to fight fiercely and after another short space of time I decided to try and get in touch with the others to see if they were alright. I rushed over to my bicycle after telling the officer in charge and jumping on rode about 100 yards up the road. *(The use of the word 'over' here is ambiguous. From where he says he was it would take him three or four minutes to get to his bicycle.)* I was, of course, seen and had only got this distance when heavy fire was directed at me, so I again dived for cover turning the bicycle into the ditch and jumping clear. After waiting a little, I crawled along till I reached the Leyland car in which, of course, there was nobody. It was in the middle of the road and about 200 yards higher up I could see the armoured car in action. *(This is wrong. The armoured car was closer to the touring car. Note that Smith says the armoured car was firing and we will see from other statements that the gun had jammed some time before.)* I crawled along until I came to a point opposite the armoured car. Then I saw the Commander-in-Chief lying wounded at the right hand side of the armoured car. Major General Dalton and Commandant O'Connell were attending him and were trying to bandage his head. General Dalton called me over with another of the party to get the Commander-in-Chief into the armoured car. We went over and as we were lifting the body I was hit in the neck. During all the time heavy firing had been kept-up. *(By whom?*

61

The IRA or Free State?) The others eventually got General Collins' body onto the armoured car which then moved down the road to the Leyland car. This was the concluding stages of the engagement which had been going on for about an hour. *(The actual duration of the fighting was ten to fifteen minutes.)* It was then nearly dusk. The armoured car pushed the Leyland and after a while the efforts of the driver to start the engine were successful. We moved on to where the tender was halted, those in the armoured car keeping up the firing all the time. *(This is rather vague. What were they firing at? Was the machine-gun firing?)* The body of the dead Commander-in-Chief was then moved onto the seat of the Leyland car and General Dalton stood there holding the body. I went to the front seat next to the driver as I had to abandon my motor-cycle. In this way we went on past the cross to Crookstown.'

After many mishaps, including the abandoning of the Leyland car, the convoy reached Cork after midnight. Lieutenant Smith's account, although not a model of accuracy, is important in so far as he describes the action at the Béalnabláth end of the ambush site.

The next published account is that of Major General Emmet Dalton, which appeared in the *Freemans Journal* on 22 August 1923, exactly a year after Collins' death. As well as being an ex-British officer with experience of writing reports, Dalton had a whole year to consider what he wrote, so one would therefore expect from him a fairly high degree of accuracy. Unfortunately such is not the case. There has, however, never been a satisfactory explanation as to why it took a full year to publish this statement. Dalton, it should be remembered, was a close friend of Collins but not everyone on the Free State side trusted him. There were many who believed that he, like Childers, was a British agent. It is true that this charge, and many other serious ones, were made against him in the public press by an erstwhile colleague. Dalton was aware of these charges but he did not take any action to have them publicly refuted. This fact did not help to allay the suspicions of his critics. Nevertheless it must be pointed out clearly that there is no solid evidence to show that Dalton was a British agent or that any of the other charges were true. I feel it necessary to emphasise this point since it has been said that I pointed the finger of suspicion at him. This is simply not correct.

Dalton's account is as follows, with my comments in italics. *(See also sketch, Appendix A)*.

'Our motor-cyclist scout was about 50 yards in front of the Crossley tender, which we followed at the same interval in the touring car. *(Collins, Dalton and two drivers were in the touring car. They were armed with rifles and Mauser pistols. The hood was down.)* Close behind us came the armoured car. We had just reached a part of the road which was commanded by hills on all sides. The road itself was flat and open. On the right we were flanked by steep hills; on the left there was a small two foot bank of earth skirting the road. Beyond this there was a marshy field bounded by a small stream, with another steep hill beyond it. About half way up this hill there was a road *(lane)* running parallel to the one we were on, but screened from view by a wall and a mass of trees and bushes. We had just turned a wide corner on the road when a sudden and heavy fusillade of machine-gun and rifle-fire swept the road in front of us and behind us shattering the windscreen of the car. *(This seems to conflict with Smith's story that the first bullets were fired at him. Also the IRA had no machine-gun.)* I shouted to the driver: "Drive like hell!" But the Commander-in-Chief placing his hand on the man's shoulder said: "Stop! Jump out and we'll fight them." *(This order of Dalton is not clear. How could they drive on when the tender was stopped in front of them?)* We leaped from the car and took what cover we could behind the little mud bank on the left hand side of the road. It seemed that the greatest volume of fire was coming from the concealed roadway *(laneway)* on our left hand side. The armoured car now backed up the road and opened a heavy machine-gun fire at the hidden ambushers. *(It is of interest that Dalton makes no mention whatever of the machine-gun in the armoured car 'jamming'.)* General Collins and I were lying within arms length of each other. Another officer, who had been on the back of the armoured car, together with our two drivers, were several yards further down the road to my right. General Collins and I, with the officer who was near us opened a rapid fire on our seldom visible enemies. About fifty or sixty yards further down the road, and round the bend, we could hear that our machine-gunners and riflemen were also heavily engaged. *(Dalton underestimates the distance here. It was nearer to two hundred yards).* We continued this firing for about twenty minutes without suffering any casualties, when a lull in the enemy's attack became noticeable. General Collins now jumped to his feet and walked over behind the armoured car obviously to obtain a better view of the enemy's position. He remained there firing occasional shots *(at what?)* and using the car as cover. Suddenly I heard him shout: "There they are running up the road." I immediately opened fire upon two figures that came into view on the opposite road *(lane).* When I next turned round the Commander-in-Chief had left the car position and had run about fifteen yards back up the road. Here he dropped into the prone firing position, and opened up upon our retreating enemies. A few minutes elapsed when Commandant O'Connell came running up the road under fire. He dropped into the position beside me and said: "They have retreated from in front of us, and the obstacle is removed. Where is the Big Fellow?" I said: "He's alright. He's gone a few yards up the road. . . Hark. I hear him firing away." Next moment I caught a faint cry: "Emmet, I'm hit." *(This is somewhat strange. How come that O'Connell did not see Collins when he came up? Was he already dead? If he was so far away that the standing O'Connell could not see him how could Dalton hear a 'faint cry'?)* We rushed to the spot with a dreadful fear clutching our heart. We found our beloved Chief and friend lying motionless in a firing position, firmly gripping his rifle, across which his head was resting. There was a fearful gaping wound at the base of the skull behind the right ear. We immediately saw that General Collins was almost beyond human aid. He could not speak to us. The enemy must have seen that something had occurred to cause a sudden cessation of fire, because they intensified their own. *(This is also strange. Does it mean that the crew of the armoured car, the two drivers, and the other officer, all stopped firing at once?)* O'Connell now knelt beside the dying, but still conscious, Chief whose eyes were wide open and normal, and whispered into the ear of the fast sinking man the words of an Act of Contrition. For this he was rewarded with a slight pressure of the hand. Meanwhile I knelt beside them both, and kept up bursts of rapid fire, which I continued whilst O'Connell dragged the Chief across the road behind the armoured car. Then with heart torn with sorrow and despair I ran to the Chief's side. Very gently I raised his head on my knee and tried to bandage his wound, but owing to the awful size of it this proved very difficult. I had not completed my grievous task when the big eyes quickly closed and the cold pallor of death overspread the General's face. How can I describe the feelings that were mine in that bleak hour, kneeling in the mud of a country road not twelve miles from Clonakilty, with the still bleeding head of the Idol of Ireland resting on my arm. My heart was broken, my mind was numbed. I was all unconscious of the bullets that still whistled and ripped the ground beside me. I think that the might of the blow must have caused the loss of my reason had I not abruptly discovered the tear-stained face of O'Connell, now distorted with anguish and calling also for my sympathy and support. We paused for a moment in silent prayer and then, noting that the fire of our enemies had greatly abated, and that they had practically all retreated, we two with the assistance of Lieutenant Smith, the motor-cyclist scout officer who had come on the scene, endeavoured to lift the stalwart body of Michael Collins on to the back of the armoured car. It was then we suffered our second casualty, the recently arrived officer *(Smith)* was shot in the neck. He remained on his feet, however, and helped us to carry our precious burden around a turn in the road and under cover of the armoured car. Having transferred the body of our Chief to the touring car where I sat with his head resting on my shoulder, our awe-stricken little party set out for Cork.' *(Dalton contradicts Smith here. He makes no reference to Collins' body being put on the armoured car and he says he sat down in the touring car while Smith says he kept standing.)* That then is Dalton's account, which as will be seen raises a few very relevant questions.

The next account is that of Private Corry, a Cheshire man, and one of the drivers of the touring car. This account was privately circulated for many years, but was published for the first time by Rex Taylor in his book *Michael Collins* in 1958.

'There were two drivers in charge of the car, M. Quinn and myself. Make of car was a Leyland Thomas Racing type, straight eight cylinder, no armour of any sort being attached at any time to bodywork or engine;

canvas top folded back to rear. General Collins and Major General Emmet Dalton were seated in the back, the two drivers in the front seat. We were aware of IRA Flying Column being about at various places during our journey down to Cork; but not a shot was fired at us. We arrived in Cork City at 10.30 p.m. — due to obstructions, blown bridges etc.

The day of the ambush. Ahead of us two Crossley tenders with ten armed men in each. Also one Crossley tender containing ropes, saws, picks, food, etc. for emergency use. *(He says there were three Crossley tenders in the convoy — the others say only one.)* Leading our column was a motor-cyclist guide. *(The word 'guide' here is a bit of a misnomer. Lieutenant Smith belonged to a Dublin brigade and had very little knowledge of the West Cork countryside.)* At the rear of our car, a Rolls Royce Whippet armoured car, named 'Slievenamon'. Two men of the convoy observed the time of departure from Bandon town as being 8 p.m. (GMT). After doing some five miles we came around a sharp curve and were then on a straight stretch of road. A single shot rang out from across the hill on our extreme left, some 440 yards away, approximately. *(This is an exaggeration. The maximum distance would be about 150 yards. It is extraordinary that Corry only heard one shot, while Dalton talks of bursts of fire which shattered the windscreen — and they were both in the same car!)* General Collins' command "Stop" was obeyed at once. *(Corry says nothing about Dalton's order 'Drive like hell'.)* There was no obstruction on the road ahead of us at the time. On leaving our car we were met by heavy fire, but no one was hit. General Collins walked back some fifty yards, followed by Major General Dalton, Quinn and myself. *(It seems incredible that they would all walk back the road for fifty yards if they were under heavy fire.)* We took cover at a hedge or ditch about two feet high. The firing was heavy at this time from enemy position right in front. On our extreme right our men were replying. On our extreme left a clear road. At our backs a steep hillside. Firing came from directly in front only. Major General Dalton observed that the armoured car machine-gun was not firing. He called to the gunner who replied, "Gun is jammed, sir." *(McPeak, the gunner, says he fired one belt of 250 rounds and the gun began to fire erratically then.)* General Collins who had been lying firing from a position six feet from me now stood erect and after firing several rounds fell on the roadside with a gaping wound near the left ear lobe extending to the upper section of the skull. There was also a tear in the front of the forehead, and a hole ripped in the front of his cap close to the badge. *(Note that Corry says the wound was on the left, while Dalton says it was on the right. Dalton also said later that there was no entry wound on the forehead or cap. Also according to Corry, Collins was standing up on the road when he was hit. Dalton says he was lying down.)* Major General Dalton said to me: "The General's finished." We placed the body across the rear of the General's car; my hands holding the head, Major General Dalton the feet of General Collins. Firing had ceased as General Collins died on the roadside. Nightfall was coming on and there was some drizzle as we started on our eighteen miles journey back to Cork.'

That is Corry's version and as you can see it differs fundamentally from Dalton's.

The next account is that of Private John O'Connell, who was one of the convoy. This account was given to Rex Taylor who published it in his book *Michael Collins* in 1958. Unfortunately Taylor did not publish it in the first person so it is hard to distinguish between what is Taylor's and what is O'Connell's. However, I can numerise the important points. O'Connell joined the convoy in Mallow to guide it to Cork. For some unknown reason he remained with the column on its tour through West Cork. He is not to be confused with Commandant Sean O'Connell.

1. According to O'Connell the touring car was in front of the Crossley tender and behind the motor-cyclist. This contradicts all the others and is obviously a mistake.

2. O'Connell got his towns completely mixed up. He says they travelled from Cork to Bandon *via Skibbereen*. Cork is 21 miles from Bandon, Skibbereen is a further 30 miles beyond Bandon. He makes the same mistake about the return journey when he says that they travelled from Skibbereen to Clonakilty *via Bandon*.

3. Presumably O'Connell was in the tender and he says they saw an old dray cart blocking the road, and came under heavy machine-gun fire. This latter was incorrect. They got out of the tender and returned the fire.

4. O'Connell states the gun in the armoured car ceased firing because two belts fell off. How did he know if he was fighting 300-400 yards away from the armoured car?

5. There was a lull in the firing, he says, and Collins stood up, looked around and started to reload his rifle. There was a single shot and Collins went down. On account of the firing it was almost ten minutes before anyone could get near his body. There was a ghastly wound near his *left* ear. At the time Collins was shot O'Connell was fighting at the very far end of the site, 300-400 yards away around a corner. How did he know all this? He couldn't possibly have seen it so we can only presume he heard it from someone else. This greatly invalidates his evidence.

6. O'Connell has one other curious remark. He says

69

that on the way the armoured car and the touring car had to be abandoned. If so then the entire convoy of more than twenty men with the body of Collins would have had to fit into the small tender. He goes on to say that two soldiers were standing guard over Collins' body all the way to Cork. It seems hard to imagine how two soldiers could stand guard over Collins in such crowded conditions, and harder still to see the purpose of them standing guard.

These are the published accounts.

One of the unpublished accounts is the version told to me by both Liam Deasy and his Adjutant Tom Crofts. Deasy's account has since been published in his book *Brother Against Brother*. They spent the day of 22 August dealing with administrative matters at the temporary headquarters of the First Southern Division of which Deasy was Commander, at Sullivans of Gurranereagh, which was close on three miles from Béalnabláth. At about 5 p.m. or 5.30 p.m., they left Gurranereagh, walking, for Béalnabláth. When they got to the village they turned out the Bandon road towards the ambush position which was about half-a-mile along this route. A short distance out they met Tom Hales and a number of other officers returning. Hales told them that he had called off the ambush and sent the protecting column home, leaving five men to remove the mine and cart. Deasy and Crofts returned to Béalnabláth with Hales and the other officers. They went into the pub for a drink and something to eat. They were there about fifteen or twenty minutes when they heard the sound of firing coming from the ambush site. They immediately rushed out and ran along the old Bandon road which is parallel to the ambush road. They then crossed a few fields and after about fifteen or twenty minutes came to high ground about 300-400 yards from the site. They could see some activity around the armoured car, although it was hazy and getting dark. They fired a few shots in that direction, but almost immediately the whole convoy moved off. They returned to Béalnabláth and after a short while the five men who carried out the ambush joined them. They reported that there were no casualties on either side. The officers then started their postponed meeting at Murray's house at about 9.30 p.m. The meeting had just begun when a scout named Sean Galvin of Crookstown rushed in and told them Collins had been killed. They were so stunned that they called off the meeting and dispersed.

Well, here you have a fair collection of statements from eyewitnesses, each contradicting the other on vital and significant points, and none of which can be accepted as a completely reliable version. When we wade through this hopeless confusion all we really know is that the convoy came under fire at Béalnabláth, shots were exchanged and Collins died. We are sure of nothing else. There would, of course, be none of this muddle had a proper inquest or inquiry been held. Under reasonable cross-examination all the various strands of disarray could be sorted out and perhaps woven into an intelligible and clear-cut pattern. We will return to this later but it is sufficient for the moment to say that the failure to hold such an inquest or inquiry was indeed a national disgrace.

We can, however, shed some light on the matter if we start by looking at the nature of the wounds on Collins' head. Several reliable witnesses, as we will see later, saw two wounds: a small entry wound on the hairline and a large gaping wound behind the right ear. Where exactly on the hairline is not clear. This entry wound was circular, symetrical and in no way jagged or torn. Could such wounds be caused by a ·303 bullet fired from a rifle at a range of 130 or 150 yards? The answer must be an emphatic 'No!' At that short range a rifle bullet would go clean through a man's head and emerge at the rear leaving a second small wound almost identical with the entry wound and totally unlike the huge gaping wound at the base of Collin's head.

Could it, however, be said that while the wounds were not caused by a straight rifle shot, they could have been caused by a ricochet off the armoured car? Indeed a ricochet could cause a large gash in the back of Collins' head but then how can the small entry wound on the forehead be explained? It might be suggested that a tiny piece of lead detached itself inside the head and then emerged through the forehead. This is certainly quite possible but if such happened this exit wound would have a jagged appearance and would cause a tear in the flesh rather than the clear, circular, symetrical incision seen by the witnesses. It seems to me therefore that any suggestion that Collins was killed by a ricochet or a ·303 rifle bullet is in no way supported by the evidence and must be regarded as fallacious.

But if he was not shot by a ·303 rifle what kind of gun would inflict the type of wounds seen by the witnesses? The most likely answer to that question would seem to be: the Mauser pistol. The barrel and the body of the Mauser pistol are in one piece and it is normally supplied with a wooden holster which can be attached to the grip of the pistol and so turn it into a mini-rifle which can be fired from the shoulder. It usually fires a 7·45 mm or 9 mm bullet which, when it strikes and enters an object, expands and tumbles and can tear the flesh to pieces inside. If the bullet emerges it usually leaves a large open wound at the point of exit. It is now considered a savage, uncivilised weapon which the Geneva Convention on war should have banned long ago, but it was widely used during and after the First World War.

The wounds seen on Collins' head are absolutely consistent with the type of bullet-wound normally inflicted by a Mauser bullet and I think it is quite reasonable to conclude that he was shot, not by a rifle, or a ricochet, but by a Mauser. This of course raises the question as to who carried Mauser pistols at Béalnabláth? The simple fact is that *some of the ambushers and some of the escort* had them and used them.

Perhaps in the light of all this we might now conclude this chapter by examining the possibility that Collins met his death through an accident of war, i.e. *that he was killed accidentally or intentionally by the IRA or accidentally by one of his own men.*

1. *The ambushers shot him by a carefully aimed shot.* This is unlikely. It is most important to understand that if the ambushers shot Collins it could only have been one of the two men whom he saw running and who were at position 10 on the sketch map *(see Appendix A)*. Collins was shot in the closing stages of the ambush, and at dusk, and by then the other three ambushers had retreated along the laneway, marked 12 on the sketch, and were both out of sight and out of range.

   To aim at and hit a small target, such as a man's head, at 130 yards with a Mauser pistol, even with the stock on, would be little short of miraculous. Theoretically the Mauser can fire up to 500 yards but there is a vast difference between the distance a bullet can carry and the distance one can get an aimed shot on target. It is also unlikely, if they were really out to get Collins, that they would have waited till dusk and the uncertainty of a Mauser bullet, when they could have picked him off earlier during daylight with a ·303 rifle — he was easily distinguishable by his prominent red and yellow rank insignia. It is unlikely, therefore, that this particular theory as to how he met his death has any validity.

2. *He could have been shot by a bullet from the section*

73

who had left the pub in Béalnabláth and who were firing from behind him. This is most unlikely. First of all the armoured car would have been directly in the line of fire and would have given him cover. Secondly, Collins was dead some time, perhaps five or ten minutes, before his party left the site, and, according to Deasy, they were only in position a minute or two when the whole convoy moved. It is, I think, reasonable to assume that Collins was dead by the time this section took up firing positions.

3. *He could have accidentally shot himself.* Very unlikely. He was found lying across his rifle with the bolt open. If he had accidentally fired a shot and killed himself the bolt would still be closed and the empty round up the breech. Also, his revolver was still in its holster.

4. *He was shot accidentally by one of his own party.* Yes. This is quite a distinct possibility. Here it is most important to realise that Collins had *never before* fought in a real ambush. Apart from the GPO in 1916 this was his first baptism of fire. Furthermore he had absolutely no training in field-craft or short range rural fighting. As well there is general agreement that he was extremely careless of his personal safety that day and was running here and there unnecessarily exposing himself to enemy fire. In these circumstances, and particularly with the failing light, it is a definite possibility that he was accidentally shot by one of his own party who was using a Mauser pistol. It has of course been suggested that most of the convoy had been drinking heavily and were in fact drunk and firing indiscriminately. I can only say that I have conducted the most thorough investigation possible into this allegation and I cannot find one shred of evidence to show that they had been drinking heavily or that any of them was drunk.

Dalton was a man with plenty of military experience and it is doubtful if he would ever have allowed such a serious lack of discipline. They were very, very tired, having been on the go since five o'clock in the morning but, as far as I can ascertain, they were not drunk. Nevertheless one must, I think, consider the likelihood of Collins being shot accidentally by one of his own men as a very definite possibility.

5. *He could have been shot by a stray bullet from an ambushers's gun fired in the general direction of the armoured car.* Yes. This could very easily have happened. The two men at position 10 on the sketch map *(see Appendix A)* were trying to retreat and as they moved they took pot shots at the convoy. One of these two was firing a Mauser pistol and was quite an experienced soldier. This man, who is long since dead, freely admitted throughout his life that he *could* have shot Collins. This has been misinterpreted so as to suggest that he did do so. But he never said that he *did so,* only that it *could* have been a bullet fired from his gun which shot Collins.

I think it is therefore reasonable to conclude that Collins could have been: (1) Accidentally shot by his own party; (2) Shot by a stray bullet fired by one of the ambushers.

However there is another version, another side to the coin, as we shall see in the next chapter.

3. Murder?

The truth would become more popular if it was not always stating ugly facts.
                                                            —H. S. HOSKINS

We have seen in the last chapter that Collins could have met his death through an accident of war caused either by his own supporters, or the IRA. Oddly enough a number of his biographers, while accepting that theory, have been careful to remark, almost as an afterthought, that there were aspects of his death not fully cleared up. They usually left it at that and did not probe any further. It was as if they were hesitant to say, what an increasing number of people have since come to suspect, that there is a lot more to the death of Michael Collins than meets the eye and that instead of being a puzzling accident it could well have been murder.

In this chapter then we will have a look at some of the suspicious elements surrounding the circumstances of his most tragic death. At the outset I would like to make it clear that this chapter does not set out to prove that Collins was murdered, but it does show that he could have been murdered, and it raises a few important, embarrassing and unanswered questions. The view that Collins might have been murdered is not held just by a small fringe group of crackbrains but by an ever-increasing body of highly responsible historians, military observers, politicians and writers. Of course the biased and bigoted tend to see this view as preposterous and fantastic because it is beyond the orbit of the little shells in which their minds are enclosed. Most great truths were once thought to be great errors. History is not only composed of ordinary conventional events and mundane happenings. More often than not it follows its own indeterminable and unpredictable course.

As a start it would be important to take a look, in so far as one can, at the mental state of Collins in the months before his death. He seemed to have reached an all-time low — dejected and disillusioned, though not despondent. 'Think what I have got for Ireland,' he said, 'something she has wanted these past seven hundred years. Will anyone be satisfied with the bargain?. . . I tell you this. . . I signed my death warrant. . . a bullet may have just as well done the job five years ago.'

And again: 'The Treaty will not be accepted in Dublin, not by those who have in mind personal ambitions under pretence of patriotism.'

For nearly a year before the Treaty was signed, as we have seen, Collins had become increasingly suspicious of De Valera's integrity, and after the Treaty all his suspicions, he believed, were fully justified. Long before the Treaty De Valera had abandoned the idea of a Republic in favour of Dominion Status — it was only a matter of how it was phrased. 'Get me out of the straight-jacket of the Republic,' he pleaded with Griffith. Now he turned about face and became a firebrand Republican. During the Treaty debates he had emphasised his constitutionalism, but he did another about face later and urged the excitable and impressionable young Volunteers to fight their brothers, not for a Republic, as he led them to believe, but for subtleties of phraseology, as Collins saw it. In Dungarvan he said: 'If you don't fight today, you will have to fight tomorrow, and I say, when you are in a good fighting position, then fight on.' This was certainly not constitutionalism.

Again in Killarney: 'In order to achieve freedom, if our Volunteers continue, and I hope they will continue until the goal is reached. . . then these men in order to achieve freedom will have to march over the dead bodies of their own brothers. They will have to wade through Irish blood.'

This kind of language was nothing more than emotional waffle, but it had a tremendous effect on thousands of young men throughout the country causing them to resort to arms and do exactly as De Valera urged. In fairness, however, it must be said that De Valera bitterly regretted these words when he saw how the Civil War developed and in a lot of his later action he tried to make amends. Indeed he was once put under arrest by the IRA for his strong views about ending the Civil War.

In the past, despite grave doubts, Collins had given unswerving loyalty to his Chief and had an absolute trust in his integrity. Now he believed that De Valera was a man of very little principle, who was prepared to twist and turn with every political wind that could be advantageous to him, in his haughty obsession with personal power.

But at least De Valera was open about it. There were others not so open. When the Treaty was passed there was an agreement that the original Republican Dáil would remain in being, and that a Provisional Government would carry on until the terms of the Treaty became law. Arthur Griffith was President of the Dáil and Collins was Chairman of the Provisional Government, in effect, Prime Minister. It has been said about Collins that he never underestimated an opponent, but that he often overestimated a colleague, and in his choice of cabinet there were two or three he did overestimate. The cabinet were: W. T. Cosgrave, Kevin O'Higgins, Paddy Hogan, Eoin MacNeill, Dick Mulcahy, Eamonn Duggan, J. J. Walsh and Joe McGrath. When men come together in a committee or in a cabinet they tend to form small power groups who for the most part consult and act together. Seemingly it gives them a greater sense of security, and this seems to have happened in Collins' provisional cabinet. W. T. Cos-grave, Kevin O'Higgins, Patrick Hogan, Dick Mulcahy, Eoin MacNeill, and somewhere in the wings the Ulster Presbyterian, Ernest Blythe, formed themselves into a kind of junta within the cabinet. McGrath, Duggan and Walsh remained outside this junta.

On the whole Collins got on reasonably well with them all except Blythe whom he really disliked. Apart from Tim Healy, Blythe must have been one of the most detested of Irish politicians. In his early days he was as extreme in his desire to shoot the British without scruple as he was later to shoot his own former comrades and friends. He was unmerciful and uncompromising in the pursuit of what were called for by the exigencies of the situation. Collins later never really trusted him and felt that his bungling was responsible for a lot of ill-will in northern Ireland.

An uncle-in-law of Kevin O'Higgins, Tim Healy, an old parliamentarian and Governor-General designate, became the mentor and adviser of this junta. They were all young, inexperienced, and in some ways, frightened men, while Healy was an old campaigner who spent most of his life involved in parliamentary and political affairs. Healy, who was a most unfortunate choice, per-suaded and convinced them that Ireland's future lay, not in an isolated Republic, but in being a good and loyal member of the British Commonwealth, and that all thought of the Treaty as a 'stepping stone' should be forgotten. Healy believed this and thought it to be in the best interests of the country as a whole, while at the same time he was not unmindful of his own personal interests. This was, of course, the direct opposite to what Collins believed and a complete reversal of the policy which underlay the signing of the Treaty. Mem-bership of the Commonwealth was for Collins a means towards a Republic, and not an end in itself.

I am afraid that in the first edition of this book I grossly under-estimated the deep divisions that existed between Collins' policies and those of the junta. Collins was heartbroken by the split and had spent months trying to bring about a reconciliation with his former comrades so that Civil War might be avoided. This group had no such scruples. They wanted Civil War long before it started so that they could crush the Republicans with all the means in their power. They had now little time for any form of Nationalism and if Ireland were to become a loyal part of the Empire then the sooner these Republicans were defeated and neutralised the better. Collins was the big obstacle in their way. They felt they had enough of his hesitancy and so they decided to push him cautiously and diplomatically to one side and move steadily towards a take-over of real power. Their motives could have been as much the saving of their own positions as the good of the country. The legality of much of what they did is open to question, but when you have a Civil War on your hands and your very existence is at stake you don't question these niceties too closely.

Their first step was to isolate Arthur Griffith, even though he had no *de jure* position in the Provisional Government, and make him ineffective on the grounds that he was sick, drinking too much and had lost touch. They openly referred to him as 'an old fogey' and even the cleaners in government buildings were rude to him. When Patrick Moylett visited him shortly before his death he found Griffith sitting alone with not even a secretary or typist available to him.

Their next step was to defuse Collins, but they did this in a different way. They persuaded him that the great priority at the moment was to win the Civil War, that he was the only one who could do it and that he should relinquish his other posts, temporarily of course, and devote himself entirely to this task. Collins fell into the trap and on 12 July 1922 he became Commander-in-Chief of the army and the junta had Cosgrave elected as Chairman of the Provisional Government in his place. So, from being effectually Prime Minister and Minister for Finance Collins was now demoted to what one might call a civil service post under Dick Mulcahy who was Minister for Defence. Collins was not now even a member of the cabinet. It is interesting to note that after Collins' death Mulcahy became Commander-in-Chief, but he did not lose his cabinet post. Why did Collins have to lose his when he became Commander-in-Chief?

It was only some short time later, but too late to change anything, that Collins found out he had been tricked by his own trusted colleagues who astutely enough kept the press and public unaware of this important change. Even to this day there are people who do not know that this happened, but all the facts can be verified by the cabinet papers now released. This was another factor weighing heavily on his mind as he made his last fatal journey to the south.

The composition of the new Irish national army, which was being recruited under the direction of Mulcahy, was also causing him a great deal of mental torment. In the months after the signing of the Treaty there was large scale demobilisation of British regiments in Ireland and instead of returning home to England, or in the case of Irishmen, returning to civilian life here, these soldiers joined the Free State army in large numbers. Emmet Dalton personally recruited many of their officers who, for the most part, were confirmed in their ranks. When British soldiers were being discharged at Colchester Barracks, England they found affixed to their discharge papers slips inviting them to join the Irish Free State army, 'where you will be heartily welcome.' Mulcahy, through his Quartermaster, Seán

Ó Muirthile, bought thousands of British army uniforms from a factory in Manchester, had them dyed green, and issued to the newly recruited soldiers.

As the Civil War progressed Collins found himself in an agonising position *vis-à-vis* this new army. Loyal and devoted comrades, his closest friends, men like Dan Breen, who at the end of his life proudly said he would gladly die for Collins, were now being hounded down and shot by the same men who had hounded and shot them during the War of Independence. These men had changed the colour of their uniform only and their leader was not now General Macready, but Michael Collins. This probably more than anything else tormented and hurt Collins and caused him the deepest mental anguish. To a friend he remarked: 'If this is to be the Free State army I want no part of it.'

As he left Dublin for the south, after Griffith's funeral, Collins was in the depths of the Dark Night of the Soul. The junta in the cabinet had settled for permanent membership of the Empire and wanted none of Collins' Republican 'stepping-stone' policies. Indeed the thing they seemingly wanted most was to get rid of him. His former comrades, now fighting against him, believed they were fighting for a Republic, but in reality they were living in cuckoo-land — they were pushing the Republic further and further away. Sections of the army he commanded, having failed to shoot down Irishmen when they were with the British, were now having a field day doing so under an Irish flag, and under his leadership. He was alone, isolated, disgusted, disappointed — the only realistic Republican of the lot.

There was a further matter playing very heavily on his mind as he sped southwards on that last fatal journey. When the Provisional Government took over Dublin Castle in the spring of 1922 Collins entrusted one of his aides, Thomas Markham, with the task of examining all the files and documents left behind in the Castle. Markham found that, while the British had removed the more recent files, they left behind a lot of documentation covering the period up to 1900. In April of 1922 he reported a startling discovery to Collins. This discovery was to the effect that James Carey had not betrayed the Invincibles in 1895; he had only given evidence against them. They were betrayed by a top political spy with the code name of 'Thorpe', and, Markham reported, 'Thorpe' was still amongst them. As a matter of urgency Collins instructed Markham to find out who 'Thorpe' really was. It took Markham four months to discover, with proof, the identity of 'Thorpe' and early in August he reported his findings to Collins. Collins was stunned. 'Thorpe' was a prominent personage high up in the Free State firmament whom Collins trusted and whose advice he had often sought on confidential political matters of the highest import — a man who was later to have a major say in the direction the new state was taking. Collins locked the file containing all this proof in his private safe at Portobello Barracks and told Markham that when he returned from his inspection down south he would deal drastically with the individual concerned. Of course Collins never returned, and when Markham tried to get the file back he found the private safe in Portobello had been opened and all files were missing. This betrayal by someone so trusted and so influential was just one more depressing thought pervading Collin's mind as he left for his journey south.

But he was not the kind of man to let despondency take possession of him as it did with the unfortunate Griffith. He possessed that supreme quality of greatness which enabled him to look the reality hard and full in the face, search for a solution and when he had found it put it into action. The first move towards any solution was to stop the Civil War, to stop the fighting, and this, without doubt was the main purpose of his journey down south. It is significant that on the morning he left, he was very sick, feverish and suffering from a heavy cold. Not only his doctor, but others who saw him, advised postponement of the journey, but he refused. Joe McGrath, one of his closest friends, did everything possible to stop him even to the extent of a stand-up row, but to no avail. Had he been going on a mere inspection trip he could easily put that off for a week or two, but it is obvious that something much more important was afoot. And that, as we now know, was the secret meeting with the neutral officers in Desmond's hotel in Cork on the night of 22 August 1922. I emphasis the word 'neutral'. Many writers have suggested that Deasy, Lynch, Breen, Hales and others were to attend the meeting. This was not so. Cork city was in the hands of Free State troops and there was no way in which any of these wanted men would come even near the boundaries. Collins was to meet neutral 'go-betweens' who had the confidence of both sides and to discuss with them terms for a cease-fire. They would then contact the IRA leaders and arrange a meeting with Collins somewhere away from the city — Hickeys of Glenville, in north Cork was the suggested venue. The matter was one of great urgency, however, and the second meeting was to be held within a few days after the first. From this second meeting it was hoped and expected that an announcement would be made calling off the Civil War.

In his book on Sir Henry Wilson, *Assassination,* Rex Taylor has a rather curious statement: 'After his death it was discovered that Collins had been guaranteed safe-conduct throughout his journey to the south and during his tour there. The document bearing this startling information was signed by a prominent anti-Treaty leader.' If this is true then it poses the question: *When were Collins' clothes searched and where is that docu-*

ment now? This question of who searched Collins' clothes and when, needs a great deal of further investigation. For example, his notebook was taken and did not turn up for forty years. He is also believed to have been carrying on his person another most important document concerning the ending of the Civil War and the merging of the two armies. This document is missing. Concerning the matter of 'safe-conduct' the Mallow IRA have stated openly that they removed all the mines from the Cork-Mallow road so that Collins and his convoy could get to Cork safely. After Cork, of course, it was no longer their problem.

If there was to be a quick cease-fire what were the terms for a settlement likely to be? Collins was now in a much stronger position to negotiate than he was a month or two previously. The IRA had been defeated in almost every battle, and they had retreated from all centres of importance, and were now simply a guerrilla force confined to the more inaccessible parts of the countryside, fighting the same type of war they had fought against the British. But this time there were three major drawbacks: 1. They were fighting against an army most of whose leaders knew as much if not more about guerrilla warfare; 2. They had no Collins to organise a vital intelligence system; 3. The ordinary people of Ireland were verging on famine conditions and wanted peace and they were simply not with them — this was probably the greatest drawback of all. Was it not the great Napoleon himself who said that he could never win a war against the civilian population?

The more responsible senior officers of the IRA realised this and also realised that it was only a matter of time before they would suffer total defeat. Dan Breen told Liam Lynch, Chief-of-Staff of the IRA: 'In order to win this Civil War you'll have to kill three out of every five people in the country and it isn't worth it.' But

Lynch was both stubborn and totally unrealistic. The thing uppermost in the minds of more responsible leaders was, apart from saving face, to save as much as possible of the Republican ideal, and indeed this was what was uppermost in Collins' mind too. When the chips were down the only real difference between them was the method to be used. Although the advantage lay with Collins he was far too noble and magnanimous to gloat in any way over the reverses of his former friends. He wanted above all peace and unity and he would approach them as a comrade and not a conqueror. His last words to General Seán Hales in Bandon that fatal day were that he did not want to injure one Irishman or even to humiliate in the least the proud spirits of those of his countrymen who may have been opposed to him.

It is not easy at this distance in time to set out with any great accuracy what the terms of settlement were likely to be. The only terms committed to paper were in a radio message from Dalton to Collins on 18 August and Collins' reply on 19 August also by radio *(See Appendix B)*. But these terms were unlikely to be very rigid and were open to negotiation, certainly in Collins' view, if not the cabinet's. The result is that all we have is hearsay which has almost certainly been twisted and garbled with the passage of time. It seems, however, Collins intended to suggest that the IRA cease fighting and join the new Irish army. If they did so he would ensure that the leaders were given the highest ranks possible and would have positions of influence and power within the army. Those leaders who did not want to join up could be accommodated in positions of importance and trust in the civil service. This would give them a powerful say in the running of the country and they would not be required to abrogate their principles by taking any oath of allegiance to the British king, since only elected representatives to the Dáil were required to do that.

Those who chose neither of these options and were in favour of continuing the fight (in other words, the diehards) could go up to the north and fight the Orangemen, who at that very moment were killing hundreds of Irish nationalists and burning thousands out of their homes. After a few years, when the new army would be well trained and equipped, the Treaty would be slowly dismantled bit by bit until it finally disappeared altogether. This, as far as I can find out, was the package Collins hoped would be accepted.

I do not know how accurate all this is, but at least it does seem a possible solution and one that is in no way inconsistent with the character of Collins. Of course, this solution poses one major question: How would the cabinet, particularly the junta, react? As I understand it this did not seem to worry Collins too much. If he could not win them over he would simply take them over. This, of course, would mean the setting up of a temporary dictatorship, until things returned to normal; again something by no means inconsistent with the character of Collins. Harry Boland once accused him to his face that he wanted to be a dictator and Collins was in no way shocked or offended, nor did he deny the allegation. Indeed it has been said that the reason Boland refused to join Collins was because he believed him a dictator and referred disparagingly to the new army as 'Collins' Green-and-Tans'. Even De Valera told the American Peter Golden that he was fearful of Michael Collins setting up a military dictatorship, but democracy or dictatorship were only words to Collins. What mattered to him was the freedom, welfare and happiness of the Irish people and he was quite prepared to try any means to achieve that end.

All this is now of pure academic interest. It simply did not happen, but it has a direct bearing on the subject of this chapter. As I have said before, Collins could at times be over-trusting to the point of precariousness. He spoke openly about the ending of the Civil War and the possibility of reunification of the IRA and the Free State army. This naturally came to the ears of the junta in the cabinet and they were well aware of what Collins had in mind, and what they suspected probably went much further. But it was not only the cabinet who knew. The British secret service knew as well.

Here we find, then, two independent bodies with a very direct interest in getting rid of Collins, *viz.*, the junta within the cabinet and the British secret service. What is of major importance here is that the IRA did not want Collins dead. On the contrary they realised he was their only hope. So let us for a moment have a look at these two groups in relation to the death of Collins.

If the junta within the cabinet wanted Collins dead could they have had him murdered, and would they have had him murdered? The answer to the first part of the question is: Yes, they could. A new detective branch with headquarters in Oriel House had just been organised and had taken over quite a number of experienced British agents most of whom could have handled a job like this without any difficulty. It would have been an easy matter to have one or two put in the Collins' escort. Indeed the reputation of some of these men became so bad that they were later disbanded and Oriel House shut down.

The answer to the question: Would they have had him murdered? seems to be — No, they would not. Collins himself never concealed his contempt for Cosgrave whom he regularly referred to as 'that bloody little altar-boy'. He detested Blythe and distrusted Eoin MacNeill and the feeling on their side was mutual, although for political reasons he had to have them in the cabinet. After his death these men made the most wonderful speeches about him, but that is the way of politicians —

the death of Collins was of tremendous propaganda value to themselves and to the Provisional Government. Even though the relationship between them was very bad it is most unlikely that it was bad enough for murder of this kind. Yet there are a lot of unanswered questions and mysterious incidents which these people could have cleared up and did not, and if the finger of guilt is sometimes pointed at them they have only themselves to blame. But, much as has been said against them, I have never heard it seriously suggested that they planned and ordered his death.

The second group of people with a particular interest in seeing Collins out of the way was the British secret service. They are and were a world-wide body operating in every country with hundreds of years of experience behind them and millions of pounds of public money at their disposal. They hold one principle, and one principle only, sacred, and that principle is: the good of the British empire. To promote this principle everything is justifiable — murder, robbery, blackmail, bribery — you name it, they know all about it. They suffered a severe set-back in Ireland at the hands of Collins who eliminated most of their agents here and they were not going to forget that. It is a basic tenet of their organisation to take revenge when one of their agents is killed — this they must do as proof to their members that no one will be allowed to get away with such killings, so it is not hard to imagine their feelings for Collins, who killed not one, but at least one hundred. No doubt they were also well aware that Collins had found out the identity of the top political spy 'Thorpe' and that he was going to take severe corrective action when he returned from Cork. They were also aware that any such action on Collins' part could have a devastating effect on future British interests in Ireland. Even if they were not actively involved in Béalnabláth the chances of Collins ever reaching Dublin were minimal. Although they suffered a severe set-back at his hands, it was only a temporary set-back. The moment the Treaty had been signed and Collins otherwise occupied, they moved back in force and penetrated almost every department of public life in Ireland, particularly the army, the new police force, and the civil service.

Indeed there is as yet no adequate study available dealing with the role of the British secret service in the Civil War. No one really knows how far their promptings were responsible for starting the Civil War or indeed for the subsequent shooting without trial of so many Republican prisoners.

In the background, but dominating everything, was the British cabinet who knew well what Collins was up to, but who could do nothing publicly to stop him so long as he remained within the framework of the Treaty. They also knew that if he were eliminated they would have no problems whatever in dealing with Cosgrave, who had now accepted fully and finally the idea of permanent membership of the British Commonwealth.

If the British secret service decided or were given orders to murder Collins how would they go about it? With such a long experience behind them they would certainly not have him picked off in the street or in his bedroom which would be too obvious. Far better to have him killed in an open engagement where the IRA could be blamed. The methods used by the British secret service are as varied as the job demands, but one of their standard procedures is to plant what is called in their parlance 'a sleeper'. In the case of Collins they would plant a man who would slowly get quite close to him and would be likely to have access to him at any time. This 'sleeper' might be years on the job, doing his ordinary work, but getting closer and closer to his victim. For security reasons he would not usually make any regular reports to his headquarters and indeed might have only very occasional contact with his bosses over a period of years. Then one day he would be told to do the job at the first available opportunity. He might be given a man or two to help him. It is not too hard to imagine how a 'sleeper' with one or two helpers could have been in the convoy at Béalnabláth. Even if there was no 'sleeper' present the carelessness with which the members of the convoy were screened would have facilitated its infiltration by secret service agents. Indeed it is now known that there were a number of changes of personnel *en route* from Dublin.

Here we have a group with a strong motive and the means of doing the job readily to hand. Those who believe in the murder theory are convinced that it was a British secret service job, but as yet there is no hard evidence to support the theory.

Let us return to the scene of the ambush once again and have a look at the IRA version of what happened. This version is a composite of statements made by some who participated in it. Two of the men I knew very well and I discussed the ambush many times with them.

All during that day it was freely rumoured among them that the war would soon be over, and as one of them said, 'We had no great mind to shoot anybody.' The very fact that an ambush was laid makes this statement difficult to understand. They put an old dray cart across the road at the Béalnabláth end of the position and a short distance further up, a mine. *(See Sketch Map, Appendix A)*. The mine was to be detonated from a position up a laneway which ran first west, and then south, parallel to the main road. About 6.30 or so it was decided to call off the ambush, as it was felt that the convoy would not return by that route. Two men were detailed to remove the cart off the road and also to defuse the mine. Three more were left behind to protect them just in case anything happened. Two of these men were at the southern side of the laneway, at a slight angle to where the monument is today. The other was about half way along that laneway at a position near two stone piers which are still to be seen. The two men detailed to clear the obstacles on the road first of all defused the mine and one of them proceeded up the laneway laden down with cables and plunger. The mine itself, defused, remained in the road until about twenty years ago when it was dug up by council workers on repair duty. The other man commenced to move the cart away. While he was engaged in this the men in the laneway saw the convoy coming. It was moving very slowly, they say, between 15 and 20 mph. There was a motor-cyclist in front followed by a Crossley tender, in which all the men seemed to be standing up. Then came the touring car and then the armoured car. After some hesitation one of the men in the laneway fired two shots, primarily to warn the man who was clearing the barricade, who immediately took cover and ran back up the laneway towards his other companion. It has been said that these two shots were fired at the roof of the touring car, but this could not be correct since the cover was completely down. The members of the convoy jumped out and took cover behind a little ditch hardly two feet high and commenced firing. The IRA say that despite their small number they had the convoy at their mercy. They had excellent cover, they were firing down on them only a short distance away and they could have picked them off one by one without difficulty. But they did not seem to want to do this. Whatever firing they did was very half-hearted, they say, and only enough to give the body of officers in Béalnabláth a chance to disperse.

The Free State party committed almost every military blunder they could. Instead of trying to hold down the IRA with covering fire while a section outflanked them, they simply ran up and down the road as if in a panic and needlessly exposed themselves. One section did attempt to move up the laneway, but the men near the piers had moved down and held them back, and even when these two men retreated the Free Staters did not exploit the advantage. After about fifteen minutes the IRA felt that the ambush had served its purpose and they retreated, three men up a small laneway to the north-west and the two other men up another small laneway to the west. It must have been these latter two that Collins saw moving when he shouted, 'There they are running,' and opened fire. These two men returned the fire for about a minute and then made good their escape. These two men say that as they were firing at an angle any bullet that hit the armoured car would ricochet away from Collins. This of course is not necessarily so. While the IRA do not deny the possibility of one of their bullets killing Collins, they say it would be one chance in a thousand since they were not aiming at anybody or anything in particular and were only holding the fort to give their officers a chance to hide. They say that the various published accounts by Free State eyewitnesses are teeming with inaccuracies and thoroughly unreliable. With regard to their fire power they say that while there were five of them there, only three of them had rifles — the other two had revolvers. They claim that Collins must have been killed either accidentally or deliberately by one of his own party.

When darkness had fallen the convoy proceeded into Crookstown and to a nearby church where the local priest refused to administer to the dead Collins. In anger one of the party tried to shoot him, but Dalton deflected the shot by striking the barrel of the rifle. The party were beset by difficulties all the way, bridges down, roads blocked, the failure of the touring car to keep going. Collins' body was transferred to the tender and the party finally reached Cork just after midnight.

Outside the Imperial Hotel, which was Dalton's head-quarters, Dr Leo Ahern, who was an Irish Army medical officer, examined the body and saw that Collins was dead and that there was nothing he could do for him. Then Dalton instructed one of his assistants, Commandant Frank Friel, to bring the body to the British Military Hospital at Shanakiel. Dalton denied this and said the body was brought to the Bon Secours Hospital. This latter is just not true. The body was never brought to the Bon Secours. Friel says he was ordered by Dalton to bring the body to Shanakiel Hospital, which was still occupied by the British, and he did as he was told. Press photographs published the following day prove Friel correct, and these reports list Dalton as being present at the removal of Collins' remains from this hospital.

At Shanakiel the troops placed guards around the hospital while the Matron, Miss Eleanor Gordon, and Frank Friel washed Collins' face and bandaged the head. According to Friel they were both quite certain that there was an entry wound on the hair-line as well as the exit wound at the back of the head. According to a statement made by the Matron, the military escort demanded that she be called in to handle the problem. As is the usual practice of hospitals the Matron never handles such cases and every emergency is handled by the nurse in charge. However at gun-point Miss Gordon was forced to take care of Collins' body. The military escort disconnected telephone communications with the outside and forbade anyone to leave the hospital. Their major concern seemed to be to prevent the news of Collins' death getting out — why this should be is hard to understand. Miss Gordon also stated that she saw a *singed* hole on the back of his tunic that looked like a bullet hole. This again is certainly mysterious. Was there another wound somewhere in his back that nobody saw? If this were a bullet hole and if it were *singed* it could mean only one thing: that the weapon which fired it must have been only a few inches away. Miss Gordon was a most reliable person who had been a military nurse in the First World War and was very familiar with such matters.

Commandant Friel, who also had experience of war injuries, believed that a rifle ·303 bullet would not have caused the gaping wound at the rear of Collins' head. He felt it was more likely that it and the entry wound were caused by a Mauser revolver bullet.

Later on Collins' remains were examined by Dr Patrick Cagney. Dr Cagney had been a surgeon in the British army during the war and had a wide knowledge of gunshot wounds. He confirmed that there was an entry wound as well as a large exit wound.

Here one must ask the tantalising question: *Why was Collins' body not brought to the North Infirmary, South Infirmary or Mercy Hospital,* all of which were nearer to the Imperial Hotel than Shanakiel? This is somewhat of a mystery since, as far as I can ascertain, all these hospitals had been taken over by the Free State army. The Bon Secours was at that time a tiny hospital used for minor illnesses only.

Another question poses itself here: *Why was it necessary to bring his body to any hospital?* He was dead and there was nothing anyone could do. Could his body not have been brought to the room in the Imperial Hotel which he occupied the previous night? On the face of it, it seems as if that would have been the more sensible thing to do.

The Cork military barracks had been burned by the retreating Republicans but there were one or two small buildings usable and in one of these Radio Officer Matt Quigley had set up a radio station some short time before. On the morning of 22 August between 12 and 1

95

a.m. he was in bed in Wren's Hotel when a messenger aroused him and requested him to report at once to Emmet Dalton. Matt dressed himself and went across to the Imperial Hotel where he met Dalton who was sitting on a couch with the chaplain Rev. Dr Scannell. General Dalton gave Matt a radio message and told him to transmit it to Mulcahy at once. The content of the message was that Collins had been killed at Béalnabláth. Matt Quigley was given a car and he went up to the barracks, which was close on two miles away, and transmitted the message. Normally radio messages were transmitted in code — a precaution against them being intercepted by British destroyers at anchor in Cork harbour. This particular one was sent 'clear' presumably there being nothing especially confidential about its content. Matt waited at the transmitter until he received, some two hours later, Mulcahy's now famous message to the army which he brought down to Emmet Dalton at the Imperial Hotel. Matt Quigley, now a retired army officer, is quite certain that he transmitted the message direct to Portobello and not via Valentia. All messages from Cork to Dublin and vice-versa were transmitted direct and there was never any question of messages being sent via Valentia or London.

In view of the fact that Matt Quigley transmitted the message at approximately 1 or 1.30 a.m. and had a reply from Mulcahy about 3 a.m. it is hard to understand why at 7.30 a.m. Emmet Dalton handed in the following telegram in his handwriting to the GPO Cork:

CHIEF OF GENERAL STAFF
DUBLIN.

COMMANDER-IN-CHIEF SHOT DEAD IN AMBUSH AT BÉALNABLÁTH NEAR BANDON 6.30 TUESDAY EVENING WITH ME, ALSO ONE MAN WOUNDED. RE-MAINS LEAVING BY CLASSIC FOR DUBLIN TODAY WEDNESDAY NOON. ARRANGE TO MEET. REPLY.

DALTON

Dalton must have known that all telephone lines between Dublin and Cork were down and all telephone exchanges smashed. Why he handed in this message is certainly puzzling.

Before we look at the question of the wound there is a further statement by an eyewitness well worth recording. In the month of March 1981, I spoke with one of the last survivors of Collins' bodyguard that fatal day in Béalnabláth and who for personal reasons would prefer to remain anonymous. He was travelling in the Crossley tender and he recalls that as they rounded a long curve on the narrow road near Béalnabláth they stopped suddenly when they saw an overturned dray cart and broken bottles barring the way. Lieutenant Smith had left his motor-cycle and was close to the barricade. As they dismounted they came under fire, not heavy, but rapid, which lasted about two minutes. They divided into two sections one of which began to remove the barricade and the other returned the fire. When the shooting ceased they could hear firing at the Bandon end of the ambush site but could not see anything as the armoured car and touring car were around the bend. After a short while the firing there stopped and the two sections moved cautiously in that direction. By the time they got there Collins was dead. It was just dusk and my informant did not see the wound. On the way back to Cork most members of the convoy showed signs of great distress, Commandant O'Connell weeping openly. At Cork they drove to the Imperial Hotel where some officer took charge of the body and brought it to the British military hospital at Shanakiel.

Three days later, in Dublin, my informant was present with Dr Oliver Gogarty, Desmond Fitzgerald, Moira Llewellyn Davies and some relatives of Collins, when Gogarty showed them the wounds. There was a large part of the flesh under the right ear blown away and Gogarty had filled the cavity with a wax-like substance. Close to the left ear there was a small circular wound which seemed 'bluish' in colour. He has further stated that this wound was clearly visible when Collins was later lying in state. My informant recollects Gogarty saying that Collins must have been shot at very close range. This man, who despite his age, impressed me very much by his anxiety to be accurate, told me that it was generally rumoured among the members of the convoy that Collins was going south to try and bring the war to an end. He also said that Dalton knew this and had in his possession details of some mined roads and some blown bridges given to him on behalf of the anti-Treaty forces as a kind of an assurance of safe-conduct and goodwill. He also said that he had seen copies of an exchange of decoded radio messages between Collins in Portobello Barracks and Dalton in Cork concerning the programme for a visit south and matters referring to conditions for a cease-fire. *(See Appendix B)*. Another thing which impressed me very much about this man's testimony was the fact that, unlike O'Connell, he spoke only of what he saw and what came within his personal experience. When I asked him a parting question, 'Who do you think shot Collins?' he answered me calmly and clearly: 'I do not know, but I am sure, as were most of my fellow soldiers, that he was not shot by the ambushers.'

This latter point is of some importance. It seems as if there was a widespread feeling throughout the Free State army at the time that the ambushers did not shoot Collins. It was openly discussed and indeed some members of the escort were subjected to embarrassing cat-calls ('Who shot Collins?') particularly on pay-nights when the drop of drink had loosened tongues.

Let us now look for a moment at this question of the wound. Dalton says it was a large gash behind the right ear, the result of a ricochet. Corry says the wound was behind the left ear as well as a wound on the forehead. Friel, Dr Cagney and the Matron of Shanakiel say there was an entry wound on the hair line. My informant saw two wounds, the large gash behind the right ear and the entry wound. He has confirmed that the entry-wound was circular, symetrical and not jagged. The noted sculptor, Albert Power, who made Collins' death mask also saw two wounds. Dr Oliver St John Gogarty, the renowned surgeon and writer, examined the body when it came to Dublin and he agreed with Dalton that the wound was a large gash behind the right ear. Many years later Gogarty, when he was living in New York, told Connie Neenan that there *was* another wound *the size of a fingernail*. The witness already mentioned saw him pointing out both wounds.

It is certainly curious that everyone, except Dalton, saw an entry wound. Dalton maintained right up to his death that there was only one wound.

There is another interesting sidelight on the question of the wound associated with Collins' cap. A cap, said to be Collins', is on public display in the Museum in Dublin. It has a large tear at the back consistent with a ricochet tearing it. This would seem to confirm Dalton's theory, except for the fact that *the cap does not belong to Michael Collins*. It is two sizes two small for him and in the interview with Cormac MacCarthaigh, Dalton stated that the cap in the Museum is his. In the Mulcahy papers there is a letter from a Dublin man named McDonnell saying that as a teenager he went to the Museum to see Collins' coat and cap when they were first put on display shortly after his death. He noticed a number of bullet holes in the cap. If this is correct then one must ask what happened to that cap? There are certainly no bullet holes in the cap on display now. Local tradition in and around Bandon and Béalnabláth says that a young girl found Collins' cap the morning after at the site of the ambush. On the advice of a priest friend she brought the cap to Bandon a week or so later and gave it to a Lieutenant in the Munster Arms Hotel (then Lee's Hotel). He subsequently gave it to General Sean Hales who was in command of the Free State troops in Bandon. Hales noticed that there was one bullet hole on the left-hand side of the band. It was this which aroused his suspicions and caused him to start probing into Collins' death. He is said to have sent the cap to Army Headquarters in Dublin as evidence of his suspicions. The cap has, however, disappeared. So again we are faced with another set of tantalising questions: *Who ripped the back out of the cap in the Museum to give the impression it was caused by a ricochet? Where is Collins' real cap and has it a bullet hole on the left-hand side of the band?* Again no answers are available to these questions.

If the British secret service were responsible for eliminating Collins and had planted a 'sleeper' or infiltrated the convoy how in fact could it be accomplished in Béalnabláth? Quite easily. Anyone near the armoured car could have shot him with a revolver using the armoured car as cover. Anyone getting close to Collins on the ground as they were firing could have shot him with a revolver. In the confusion of the ambush and the fading light such a shooting could pass unnoticed. This in fact is what happened, say those who believe in the murder theory. He was shot, they claim, by a British secret service agent and the IRA were blamed. But, of course, there is no real proof. It should be noted that the exact position of Collins when he was struck by the bullet is unknown. Whether he was standing or lying down, or where he was is uncertain. Here again one sees the disastrous results of no inquest having been held.

In the *Daily Express* for 25 August 1922 there is a most curious news item. Apparently the Dublin correspondent interviewed one of the escort who says that he was close to Collins. '. . . *He noticed a sniper creeping up on hands and knees down the road behind him. Mick (Collins) went a dozen yards in that direction. There was a sudden burst of firing. Mick turned and fell.'* It seems as if this news item never came in for any serious or critical examination in the past and of course it is too late now to pursue it.

Commencing in May 1968 Cormac MacCarthaigh wrote a series of articles in the Irish language magazine *Agus* casting grave doubts upon Emmet Dalton's statements and raising many baffling questions. These articles led to an interview between the two which was published in *Agus* in July 1970 and through the kindness of the Editor and of Mr MacCarthaigh I am permitted to publish the text of this interview in full. I have put my own comments in italics.

MacCARTHAIGH: I thank you for agreeing to talk with me on this subject.

DALTON: I have constantly refused to comment on this phase of our history though I have had several offers and requests. Regarding the death of Collins, I have made my report which was published. This was a military report and correct. You have stated that there are inaccuracies in the report and that is what makes me interested.

(I do not think Dalton's report could be classified as a 'military' one. It is far too incomplete and I imagine any self-respecting Commanding Officer would have sent it back to him for completion. He seems to suggest that because a report is 'military' it must be accurate. This is not necessarily so. The great Marshal Foch said he never believed more than fifty-per-cent of any military report.)

MacCARTHAIGH: For example you refer to one of the reasons for Collins' visit to Cork on 20/8/22 as 'in his capacity as Chairman of the Provisional Government'.

101

Collins had ceased to be Chairman of the Provisional Government six weeks previously. Did you know at the time you wrote the report that this was so?

DALTON: No. I never heard it. Are you sure that is correct?

MacCARTHAIGH: Absolutely. The evidence is extant.

(It is hard to credit that Dalton did not know this. Admittedly it was not made public, but since he was such a confidant and close friend Collins would have told him and discussed the implications.)

MacCARTHAIGH: How well did you know Collins?

DALTON: Very well. I adored Collins. He was the greatest Irishman of all times. He worked for sixteen hours out of twenty-four and expected everyone else to do the same.

MacCARTHAIGH: Was it an error of judgment on his part to have signed the Treaty?

DALTON: We have to judge this issue on the known facts of the time and not on hindsight. Collins was right in signing the Treaty — there was no alternative. We could not have held out much longer in Dublin. We were terribly short of fighters because of arrests and casualties, and had little hope of getting any. We tried to get men from the country, but they were too easily identifiable and were picked up too easily. In any case fighting areas of the country were short too. More than 120 men took part in the attack on the Custom House 25/5/21. Most of them were captured and put under military guard outside the Custom House itself while it was blazing. The detectives from the Castle were able to identify many of these men who took part in the Bloody Sunday operations and they would all have been shot at once. They shouldn't have taken part in this operation, but we had no one else. With Christy O'Malley, Adjutant Dublin Brigade, and Maurice Walshe I searched the whole of Dublin to see if I could get three or four men who would set up a diversionary attack in Marlborough Street to draw off some of the

British forces from the Custom House, so as to give the prisoners a chance to make a break and we failed to get even one. We had to send men into the Custom House who should not have been there at all — men who had taken part in the Bloody Sunday shootings and who were known to Dublin Castle. They would not have stood a chance if captured. That was how things were with us in Dublin after the Custom House. I would not like it to be thought that I am finding fault with the Custom House operation, a scheme which was devised by political chiefs and deputed by them to the C/O Dublin Brigade. Under the command of Tom Ennis the Second Battalion carried it out with the assistance of the Active Service Unit, the Squad and other small units. I believe the operation achieved its objective and helped the peace offer from the British.

MacCARTHAIGH: At the meeting at which Cosgrave replaced Collins as Chairman of the Provisional Government a committee of three was appointed to prosecute the war — the members being Collins, Mulcahy and O'Duffy. Mulcahy was both Minister for Defence and Chief-of-Staff, and Collins was titled Commander-in-Chief? How could it work?

DALTON: In England the Commander-in-Chief is the Queen; in the USA the President is the Commander-in-Chief, but the Chief-of-Staff gives the orders. In our case in 1922 we were evolving from a part-time Volunteer force with whole-time guerrilla units to a professional army. *(This answer is not too impressive.)*

MacCARTHAIGH: Were you aware of difficulties between Collins and other members of the Provisional Government?

DALTON: No, and I do not believe that there were.

MacCARTHAIGH: Both O'Higgins and Hogan were mentioned as being anti-Collins.

DALTON: This is not true. Both of them were very strong

supporters of Collins.

MacCARTHAIGH: Who to your knowledge would be anti-Collins?

DALTON: Only one to my knowledge and then I do not know how much he disliked Collins. I do know that Collins had no time for him because of his handling of things in the north, and that Collins had told him so in no uncertain terms as Collins could. *(This man referred to here was Ernest Blythe.)*

MacCARTHAIGH: Did Collins meet any neutral members of the IRA to consider peace while in Cork?

DALTON: He met several people, but I do not know who they were. You must remember I had a job to do.

(Dalton was with Collins all the time in Cork and met these people with him. It is hard to credit that Collins did not introduce them and tell Dalton who they were. According to documents in the Mulcahy papers, and in private hands, on 11 August 1922 Dalton received representations to transmit to Collins suggesting a week's truce. See Appendix B. He transmitted these terms to Collins by radio on 18 August. I think he is not being quite straight in denying all knowledge of peace moves and who Collins met. As we have seen the survivor of the convoy whom I interviewed actually saw copies of these proposals which passed between Collins and Dalton over the radio.)

MacCARTHAIGH: Did you meet Sean Hegarty?

DALTON: I do not know.

MacCARTHAIGH: What was the object of Collins' visit to West Cork?

DALTON: He wanted to meet Sean Hales in Bandon, his brother and other relatives.

(It is hard to credit that almost everyone in the party except Dalton knew that the main purpose of his visit to West Cork was to contact the IRA and bring the war to an end.)

MacCARTHAIGH: Did Collins' meet any 'Irregulars' at White's public house at the Pike outside Clonakilty?

DALTON: He met several civilians whom I understood to be relatives. In fact I do not know who they were. Collins did not say. He did not discuss any matter other than of a military nature with me.

(This is very hard to accept. Dalton spent two days sitting in the same car with Collins and he would have us believe they never spoke to each other except on military matters. He is certainly not being very open.)

MacCARTHAIGH: When you left Bandon on the return journey where were you going?

DALTON: Back to Cork. I advised against returning by the route which we had come, but I was over-ruled. *(Whom did he advise and by whom was he over-ruled?)*

MacCARTHAIGH: The motor-cyclist Smith stated in an interview the following day that you were returning to Macroom that evening. You had been to Macroom that morning and also on the previous day. Had these visits to Macroom any political significance?

DALTON: None whatever. *(How did he know if he only discussed military matters with Collins?)*

MacCARTHAIGH: Was Collins trying to make contact with the 'Irregulars' headquarters to the west of Macroom?

DALTON: Not as far as I know.

MacCARTHAIGH: In your report on Béalnabláth you stated that 'a heavy fusillade of machine-gun fire swept the road.' There were only four men on the other side.

DALTON: This is what is being said now, but there must have been at least six to eight there — at least six. Even after Collins had been hit we were still being sniped.

MacCARTHAIGH: Commandant Frank Friel has said that the wound at the base of the skull was an exit wound, and that an entrance wound at the edge of the hair on the forehead was discovered in the hospital. This entrance wound appeared to him to be made by a

Mauser pistol which would account for the large gaping exit wound.

DALTON: Friel was wrong in this. Collins' head was resting on my arm on the rear seat of the car for part of the journey back so I should know.

(Five other people besides Friel saw a second wound so according to Dalton they were all wrong. How could Dalton be so certain if it was pitch dark in the car?)

MacCARTHAIGH: Who selected the escort party?

DALTON: I do not know. It was the escort party which came from Dublin and I certainly would not have selected them. They knew nothing of conditions in the country. I had a good acquaintance with West Cork because as officer in charge of training I had travelled all over it with Tom Barry during the Truce. *(But Dalton could easily have changed the whole escort party in Cork.)*

MacCARTHAIGH: It has been said that the officers including Collins were drunk.

DALTON: This is false.

MacCARTHAIGH: Did you get a priest for Collins?

DALTON: On the road we came to a church with a gravel patch in front and iron railings on the roadside. One of my men went in for a priest. A priest came out to the railings, looked at the body of Collins lying on my arm on the rear seat of the car, turned around and walked away. One of the officers raised a rifle to shoot him and only that I struck the rifle out of his hands the priest would have been shot. The shot actually went off. This action by the priest had a very serious effect on the morale of my men. Apart from a complaint to the Rev. Dr Scannell the following day I have never mentioned it since.

(I have investigated this incident and as far as I can find out the unfortunate priest was one of those people allergic to the sight of blood and when he saw Collins' head he put

his hands over his face and backed away.)

MacCARTHAIGH: I have heard that story and wished to have it checked.

DALTON: I did not know it was known. I did not wish to circulate it. Do you know the name of the priest? I have never heard.

MacCARTHAIGH: Yes. You left the body on the Western Road in Cork with instructions that it had to be taken to the British Military Hospital.

DALTON: I had to return to the Imperial Hotel (G.H.Q.) to report the matter, but my recollection is that the entire party went there and that Dr Leo Ahern took the body to the Bon Secours Hospital. Colonel Ben Byrne agrees with me and in our opinion Frank Friel is wrong.

(Frank Friel was in fact right. The body was never in the Bon Secours Hospital, but was brought by Friel on Dalton's instructions to the British Military Hospital at Shanakiel.)

MacCARTHAIGH: What was the cause of the delay in getting back to Cork from Béalnabláth — a distance of only nineteen miles?

DALTON: We had to take back roads because of trees felled and trenches cut on the main roads. At one point we had to drive through a haggard over a ditch and out through a paddock gate. This was a nightmare with heavy transport, particularly the armoured car.

MacCARTHAIGH: How was it that the *Freemans Journal* and the *Daily Express* carried a full account of Collins' death that morning and the *Cork Examiner* did not?

DALTON: I had nothing to do with that. I simply reported that matter to Dublin. I had a wireless link with the cable station in Valentia and from there the message was cabled to New York and then back to London and from there to Dublin. I was amazed to get a cablegram later that morning addressed to 'Commanding Officer, Cork' from Hearst Newspapers New York offering one thousand dollars for the Collins' story.

(This is rather extraordinary. Matt Quigley, who actually transmitted the message, is quite certain that he sent it direct to Dublin, and he is also certain that there was no question of the message ever being sent via Valentia, New York and London.)

MacCARTHAIGH: A military cap has been on display in the National Museum as being the cap worn by Collins at the time of his death. It appears to me that the cap in question is too small to have been worn by Collins. In the 'blow-up' of the photographs taken of Collins shortly before his death the position of the cap badge does not agree.

DALTON: It is probably my cap. I put my cap under his head to contain the wound. *(The answer does not explain the large tear at the back band of the cap in the Museum.)*

MacCARTHAIGH: You left the army shortly afterwards?

DALTON: Yes. That is correct, but I do not wish to discuss the reasons publicly. I have never done so and I do not think it right that I should do so now.

(This is the end of the interview. A few months after Collins' death, Dalton resigned from the army and was appointed by the cabinet to a top job as Clerk of the Senate. One version says he was strongly opposed to the execution of prisoners, refused to carry out such executions, and as a protest resigned. Apart from the fact that the Republicans would not go along with this version, it is unlikely that if it were true the cabinet would have given him the plum job in the Sentate. The second version says that after Collins' death he became weary and disillusioned with the Civil War and asked to be relieved. This version seems more likely. Up to the end of his life he spoke regularly of his deep love and admiration for Collins. He was an intelligent man and if he later felt that his mistakes at Béalnabláth were even remotely responsi-

ble for the death of his hero he could very easily have taken this to heart and allowed it to affect the course of his life. He did not stay long in the Senate job and after a career of ups and downs, mostly abroad, he died in 1978. It was said that during the Second World War he joined MI5 but there is no hard evidence of this and his close friends deny it absolutely. They say he worked in films in England during that period.)

Again a few months after Collins' death, John McPeak, the gunner in the armoured car, deserted to the IRA and brought the armoured car with him. There are also different versions as to why McPeak deserted. One says he was disgusted with the shooting of prisoners, particularly that of Timothy Kennefick, a captain of the IRA, who was beaten unconscious and then shot at Coachford by Free State troops. Another version says he became emotionally involved with a young girl of Republican sympathies in West Cork, while a third says he was constantly being accused by his fellow soldiers of shooting Michael Collins and he was terrified for his life. This latter is of some importance for it shows again that the ordinary rank-and-file within the army did not accept the story that Collins was killed by the IRA. The survivor to whom I spoke confirmed that this view was prevalent. Whatever the reason was he changed sides and brought the armoured car with him. All he asked from the IRA was that they smuggle him back to his native Scotland and give him a few pounds. This they succeeded in doing after a short delay.

In July 1923, McPeak was picked up by the Scottish police and extradited to Ireland where he was put on trial for the larceny of an armoured car. He was sentenced in the Irish courts to five years in Portlaoise jail. He was released in August 1928, having spent most of his time in solitary confinement, and then disappeared to England where he started a new life under an assumed name. It is fairly certain that McPeak did not shoot Collins. He was very devoted to him and had worked for Collins in Scotland long before the Treaty. If he were a British secret service 'sleeper' they would certainly not have let him be picked up later by their own police and handed over to the Irish police, even if it were only to ensure that he kept his mouth shut. On the contrary, they would have seen to it that he got a good job and was well looked after. This is a fundamental part of their code.

There is however one curious factor in this whole McPeak saga. He deserted to the IRA three months after Collins' death bringing the armoured car and a machine-gun with him. It is rather strange that at his trial he was charged only with the larceny of an armoured car and machine-gun. *He was not charged with desertion*. Why? Could it be that if he were charged with the wider charge of desertion a lot of what happened at Béalnabláth would come out in evidence and could be a serious embarrassment to the Government? Unfortunately this is one of the many questions to which we have as yet no answer. However, McPeak is reputed to have left some important documents after him and when these are made public they may give us a clue. Before he died, however, he made a rather important revelation. He said that his assistant machine-gunner was changed in Cork the evening before and replaced by a stranger whom he did not know. Why was this? Again no answer is available.

Seán Hales, who commanded the Free State troops in Bandon was highly suspicious of the whole account of the Béalnabláth ambush. Because it happened in his area he tried to have all the participants brought back to Bandon so that he might hold a proper court of inquiry. He failed to get the necessary permission to have this done. Nevertheless, he continued making inquiries and on his next visit to Dublin he contacted army headquarters and members of the cabinet, expressing his grave doubts and demanding that a proper court of inquiry be instituted into all matters pertaining to Collins' death, as he did not accept Dalton's version, which had only been given verbally and not yet published. He was met with a blank refusal everywhere. His driver and constant companion, Jim Woulfe, has confirmed all this many times and in a letter to me said: . . . *after Michael Collins was killed at Béalnabláth I was appointed as General Seán Hales' driver by Captain Davy Coats who at the time was in charge of armoured-cars in Cork. Hales was allotted a Lancia armoured-car for West Cork. During the time I was driving him his chief topic of conversation was Michael Collins. He told me that he would leave no stone unturned until he got an inquiry or inquest held on Michael's death. . . At this time he was about three times in Dublin but all to no avail. The 'big brass' in Dublin would not listen to him. He told me so himself and I can assure you he was a very disappointed man.*

As an army officer Hales normally stayed in Portobello Barracks when he was in Dublin. On one of the last evenings there he was told that they had no accommodation available for him, so he had to move to a hotel. The next day as he travelled in a side-car from his hotel with Padraic Ó Maille he was attacked and shot dead. The IRA have consistently denied that they had anything to do with this shooting. It has been suggested that Hales knew too much and the British secret service had to stop him. In his book *The Singing Flame* Ernie O'Malley suggests that the IRA shot Hales as part of a policy to shoot all who voted for the Execution Bill in the Dáil. First of all Hales did *not* vote for the Bill as he was absent. Secondly O'Malley was in jail at the time and did not really know what was happening outside. The man who did know what was happening in Dublin was Moss

Twomey, one of the IRA officers in charge of the city. Twomey always maintained that no orders whatever were given to shoot Hales and it was not the IRA's doing. Hales was supposed to have been shot by two men who then ran away. Yet the driver of the side car did not say he saw these two men. Neither did the various people passing the hotel at the time. In fact the only person who said he saw the two men was a British soldier. This soldier, together with an officer, were seen by others, near the hotel, with their guns drawn. At the inquest the only evidence that two men shot Hales came from the soldier.

Another rather unusual thing happened on the day of Collins' death. Max Aitken (Lord Beaverbrook) who was then running the *Daily Express,* sent over a Canadian journalist shortly after the signing of the Treaty and told him to stick around Collins. 'There will always be news in that fellow,' Aitken said. True enough the journalist sent many interesting stories about Collins back to his paper. But on 22 August, time unknown, he telephoned the *Daily Express* and asked them to hold the main page for an important item of news. His contacts, he said, could not tell him what the news was except that it was of top-importance. They held the space and then in the early hours of 23 August he was able to telephone his paper that Collins had been shot at Béalnabláth.

All that has been said in this chapter does not prove that Collins was murdered. All it shows is that it could have happened, but what it does indicate is that there are an awful lot of unanswered questions and uneasy doubts. Perhaps if I assemble some of them here it would be a fitting end to the book.

THE ESCORT

Michael Collins was the most important man in Ireland at the time, and because of the number of British agents whose deaths he was responsible for as well as the hazards of a Civil War, he was particularly vulnerable to an attempt on his life. There is evidence in the State Papers that during the Truce he was regularly followed by British secret service men. Consequently, the greatest care should have been taken in choosing any escort for him and each member of that escort should have been thoroughly screened. As we have seen that was not done. They seem to have been selected haphazardly, and there were many ex-British soldiers in their ranks. There was some chopping and changing as well *en route*. In circumstances like this it would not have been difficult for a British secret service agent with forged papers to have infiltrated the convoy. We do not know who was responsible for choosing that escort, but we do know that nobody was ever formally charged with negligence in so choosing.

THE ROUTE

There has been no satisfactory explanation of why so many visits to Macroom were necessary within the space of twenty-four hours, but these visits must have some significance. Collins could have returned to Cork by the normal route as the bridge at Innishannon was temporarily fixed; he could have returned via Kinsale or via Crossbarry or indeed, according to Deasy, by four other routes. Assuming then that he had something important to attend to in Macroom why did the convoy not go the direct Bandon – Macroom road? Instead they went via Newcestown, Béalnabláth, a round-about way with probably more dangerous ambush sites per mile than any road in Ireland. Again why did they commit the cardinal military offence of returning by the same route they came? The important question is, however, who chose this route? Collins was not acquainted with the area around Bandon and while he probably made the decision to go to Macroom it is unlikely that he chose the exact route. Who did then? Was it Dalton who said that he knew West Cork well; or was it someone else who suggested it?

THE AMBUSH

It is hard to understand why Dalton did not at least try to rush Collins to the armoured car immediately it came up to them. There he would have had perfect protection. The armoured car could then have been driven back the Bandon road for half-a-mile or so and stayed there in safety for twenty or thirty minutes until darkness fell. The function of the escort was to *protect* Collins, not to fight a battle with the IRA, and it was not the function of a General and a Commander-in-Chief to lie down on the side of the road and expose themselves to enemy fire. There seems to have been no one in real command and everyone seemed to do as they wished. Lieutenant Smith, for example, rushed all of 500 or 600 yards from where he had been fighting to where Collins was and it is hard to see much sense behind that move. Again the machine-gun in the armoured car failed to function properly. This can happen at the best of times, but according to a later statement by McPeak it happened frequently with this particular gun. One cannot help wondering why a man of Collins' importance was given an unreliable machine-gun for protection. Again one must wonder who was really in command? Collins was only a passenger to be protected.

THE WOUND

Several people stated they saw a second wound and while it is reasonable to assume that one or two could make a mistake it is hard to credit that all could be wrong. This makes it all the more difficult to understand Dalton's insistence, even up to the time of his death, that there was only one wound, and that wound was caused by a ricochet. He must surely have seen many such wounds caused by Mauser pistols as these were used in the main by German officers in the First World War, and Dalton had considerable experience of front-line fighting. It is understandable that he might not have seen the small entry wound in the darkness on the return journey to Cork, but he was one of the pall-bearers the following day at Shanakiel Hospital and must have seen Collins' body laid out. I have learned recently that it was common knowledge in Government circles in Dublin that there was an entry wound somewhere on the hair line which was quite visible as Collins lay in state. It is also curious that Oliver Gogarty waited forty years before he stated publicly that there was an entry wound. If what Miss Gordon saw was a bullet wound in the back did anyone know of it?

Again the affair of the cap is not without suspicion. Where is Collins' real cap? Who ripped the back band on the cap in the Museum to make it look as if caused by a ricochet bullet? Would Collins' real cap show an entry bullet hole?

THE AFTERMATH

Michael Collins was killed in circumstances open to many different interpretations. Senior army officers, like Major General Seán Mac Eoin, Major General Seán

Hales and historians like Donn Piat expressed the gravest doubts about the official version of his death. I learned recently, from a most reliable source, that Desmond Fitzgerald, who was a cabinet minister, spoke openly to his friends about his doubts concerning the official version and certainly on one occasion made a definite statement as to what happened. The rank-and-file of the army spoke openly of his being murdered. Yet despite all this unease the normal process of law was put to one side and no coroner's inquest was held.

If an inquest had been held on Collins there would be no speculation as the cause or manner of his death. Firstly the exact cause of death would have been determined. If one wanted to engage in a flight of fancy one could say that there is no evidence to show that Collins did not die of a heart attack, or that he was not poisoned and that the wounds were not inflicted afterwards. As matters stand there is no real evidence to show what caused his death, and we can only presume it was caused by gunshot wounds. If a proper inquest had been held all members of the escort would have been cross-examined and this would have determined the exact details of the ambush and of the events leading up to it. What drink was consumed *en route,* the sobriety of the officers and men, the reason for taking the Béalnabláth road, the composition of the escort, the tactics adopted when fired upon and all other relevant details would have come out in the open. As well, the medical evidence would have determined the location and number of wounds, whether or not what Miss Gordon saw was a bullet wound, the calibre of the bullet, the direction from which it came and the distance at which it was fired. If such an inquest had been held there would be no mystery whatever surrounding Collins' death. This of course tempts the question: *If everyone were absolutely certain that the IRA shot Collins would there have been an inquest?*

But why was there no inquest? Ernest Blythe was one of those who regularly produced an old chestnut of an answer. He said there was a war on and an inquest could not be held on everyone who happened to get shot. Yet inquests were held on Cathal Brugha, Harry Boland, Seán Hales, Liam Lynch, Colonel McCurtain, Colonel Collison and a host of others who died from gunshot wounds. An examination of the provincial newspapers of the period shows that inquests on soldiers as well as officers killed in action were a commonplace feature of the daily news. This answer of Blythe cannot be taken seriously and can only be seen as a rather lame adjunct to the whole cover-up.

Another excuse put forward is one which says that inquests are entirely a matter for coroners to act according to their own discretion. If this is so then it is extraordinary that the coroners of Cork held so many inquests on soldiers killed in action during that particular period and missed out on Collins. I find this excuse rather hard to accept and I think one must dig a little deeper to try and find the answer.

A few weeks after Collins' funeral when Seán Hales was unsuccessfully campaigning to have an inquest, or at least an inquiry held into Collins' death there appeared in the *Cork Examiner* a rather strange advertisement. *Inter alia* this advertisement said:

> *Now I, the undersigned, being the competent military authority for the County of Cork, hereby order that no inquest shall be held in the said County unless written authority for the holding of same shall have been first given by me.*

This extraordinary advertisement was signed by none other than Major General Emmet Dalton.

The excuse Dalton gave for suppressing inquests in

Cork was that jurors were being intimidated. This may well have been so, but it is somewhat strange that such intimidation seems to have been confined to Cork only. I cannot find any newspaper record of the other military commanders in different parts of the country having to take such serious action. If the IRA were intimidating jurors in Cork surely one could expect them to do likewise in Kerry, Tipperary, Clare, Limerick and other counties.

But the importance of this advertisement is not so much in the fact that it suppressed the holding of inquests in Dalton's territory as in the fact that it proves Dalton had absolute power over inquests in the whole Cork area. If he could suppress an inquest surely he could initiate one. As the 'competent military authority' he could have ordered an inquest to be held into the death of Collins. Why he did not do so is just another unanswered question in the whole mysterious saga.

Collins' body was brought to Shanakiel, a British military hospital, not yet handed over and still manned by British personnel. Why was he not brought to any one of three Irish hospitals, the Mercy, the South Infirmary or the North Infirmary which were nearer, is still unexplained. Also unexplained is Dalton's insistence, up to his death, that Collins was brought to the Bon Secours, when there are press photographs and abundant other evidence to show that he was brought to Shanakiel. Whether or not the doctors carried out an autopsy there is unknown. But if an autopsy was carried out the results are missing — presumably destroyed with all the other Collins' documents by order of Desmond Fitzgerald just before Fianna Fáil took office in 1932. In an action such as Béalnabláth, where the Commander-in-Chief was killed, a full military inquiry, would, under normal circumstances, take place at once. This inquiry would examine and report on the whole military aspects of Collins' death. It would examine the purpose of his visit to the south, the composition of his escort, the routes taken, the military response to the attack, the manner of his death and every factor even remotely bearing on the ambush. Such an inquiry would allocate blame, if any, and recommend court-martial proceedings where necessary. But there was no formal inquiry of any kind, despite every effort of Major General Seán Hales to have one instituted. Why such an inquiry was never carried out remains still unexplained. It has been suggested to me that some kind of a private inquiry was held by the army. I cannot find a shred of solid evidence to support this suggestion. None of the escort with whom I spoke were questioned in any formal way or asked to attend an inquiry. If such an inquiry were held what were the results? Where are those documents now? Why have they never been made public?

Finally there is the mystery of the Collins' documents, previously mentioned, which were burned a few days before Fianna Fáil took office in 1932 by orders of the then Minister for Defence, Desmond Fitzgerald. According to a private statement made by one of the military personnel who actually did the burning, these documents contained, among other things, details relevant to the execution of prisoners by the Free State army, the composition of the courts' martial and the names of the firing squads. He also noticed a very large well-bound file or folder which contained a lot of documents concerning Michael Collins. Some of the Collins material was typewritten, some handwritten, but he was given no chance of reading it. When everything was burned, he said, the ashes were raked and carted away.

It has been generally believed that the Collins documents burned contained all his confidential files relative to the Civil War including the Markham file on the identity of 'Thorpe', Gogarty's autopsy report and other secret letters and reports concerning Collins' death. This particular charge concerning the burning of documents has been published on and off in books and newspapers over the past twenty years yet neither the Government, the Army, nor the Fine Gael party have contradicted it. Perhaps it was because he had read those Collins' files that Desmond Fitzgerald doubted the official version. *If there was nothing to hide why were the documents burned?*

As I came to the end of this book, having unsuccessfully tried to sift all the evidence, two rather important questions remained in my mind. To resolve these I contacted an acquaintance who had given a lot of study to this matter and who was firmly convinced that Collins was murdered, and put the questions to him.

My first question, assuming that Collins was murdered, was: *Collins was a very shrewd man. How did he let himself be fooled by a British secret service 'sleeper'?* His answer was: 'Yes, he was a shrewd man, but he was also a man of great likes and dislikes. If he liked someone he tended to trust that person. The British secret service knew that and they cleverly exploited this trait. It was also no problem to them to infiltrate the convoy. It would be going a little too far to say that Collins could not be deceived. Such a claim can be made for no man.'

My second question was: *If the British secret service killed Collins why did the Irish government co-operate by suppressing information etc.?* 'Within a day or two of Collins' death,' he answered, 'some of the officers and men of the convoy who were loyal to him found out about the murder and immediately contacted government headquarters in Dublin. The government decided that at all costs they must suppress this information from becoming public. If it were generally known that the British killed Collins the government feared there

120

would be a strong anti-British, and consequently anti-Treaty, backlash and this could prove to be of tremendous advantage politically to De Valera and his followers. They, therefore, decided to suppress it, not to protect the British secret service, but to protect themselves. This explains why there was no inquest, no inquiry and why documents were ultimately destroyed. Even apart from all that, to be able to blame Collins' death on the IRA was of tremendous propaganda value to the government in winning the Civil War.'

Whatever one may think of these answers there is no doubt but they are both interesting and intriguing. I presume similar reasons for a cover-up could be advanced if the shooting was thought to be accidental.

It is nearly sixty years now since Michael Collins died on that lonely roadside in west Cork and there is little hope at this late stage of fully piecing together the complicated jigsaw of his death. There are sane and balanced people who believe he was murdered as there are sane and balanced people who believe he was not. Almost everyone who took part in that tragic ambush is dead and any kind of inquiry involving eye-witnesses is now out of the question. But there is one thing which can be done even at this late hour. The government could exhume the body of Collins, which was said to have been embalmed by Oliver Gogarty before burial, and have an autopsy carried out. This would establish clearly what kind of a wound was inflicted on his head and what kind of a bullet killed him as well as the range from which it was fired. This could go a long way towards solving this durable and bewildering mystery. I think, not only the government, but we the people, owe at least that much to the greatest Irishman of a thousand years.

APPENDIX A

All positions indicated are approximate.

1. Cart across road.
2. Mine.
3. Crossley tender stopped here.
4. Touring car stopped on bend and occupants moved back towards armoured car.
5. Armoured car.
6. Point at which Collins died.
7. Position of Section who arrived from Béalnabláth.
8. Laneway which could have been used by armoured car for infiltration.
9. Laneway by which two IRA at 10 retreated.
10. Corner from which retreating IRA fired.
11. Two piers of gate from near which IRA were firing on Crossley tender.
12. Laneway by which three IRA men retreated.
13. Free State troops came up laneway to approximately this point.
14. Entrance to laneway.

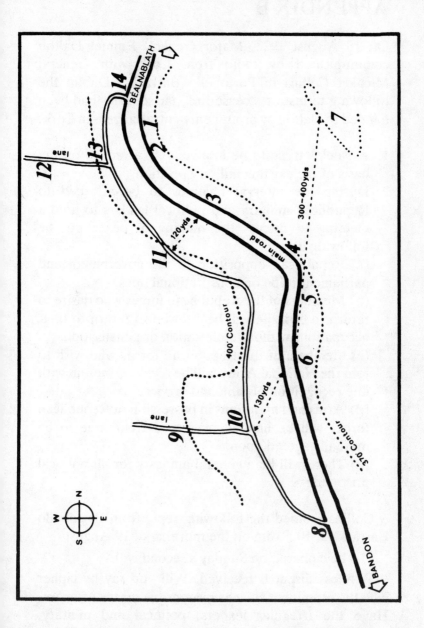

BÉALNABLATH

14

1

2

3

main road

4

5

6

7

300–400yds

11

120yds

400' Contour

13

12 lane

10

130yds

9 lane

370' Contour

8

BANDON

N
W · E
S

APPENDIX B

On 18 August 1922, Major General Emmet Dalton communicated by radio from Cork with General Michael Collins in Portobello Barracks, Dublin the following terms for a cease-fire. These terms had been handed to Dalton by prominent neutral citizens in Cork.

1. A week's truce to be immediately arranged on the basis of the existing military position.
2. During the interval facilities to be afforded to Republican military and political leaders to hold a meeting to discuss the making of peace on the following basis:

   (a) Republican opposition to the government and parliament to be on constitutional lines.

   (b) Members of the Republican forces who desire to return to civil life will be allowed to return to their occupations without molestation or penalisation.

   (c) Members of the Republican forces who wish to join the National Army will be received therein with due recognition of rank and service.

   (d) Arms and munitions in possession of Republican forces will be handed over to a committee to be mutually agreed upon.

   (e) There will be a general amnesty for all political prisoners.

Collins radioed the following reply from Portobello Barracks at 10.50 am on the morning of 19 August:

(To be ciphered on Sunday's second word)

Wireless dispatch received. Will you say by cipher who the prominent citizens responsible for the offer are. Have the Irregular leaders, political and military, agreed to the offer and is it made on their behalf?

Government offer published in the press 5th June, and conveyed to the Peoples Rights Association, Cork, stands. For your guidance the terms are:

First: Transfer into the National Army of all war materials.

Second: Restoration, without exception, of all seized property and money.

Third: Particulars be furnished of bridges, railways, roads which are or have been mined or rendered otherwise unsafe.

Commander-in-Chief

These terms were, of course, merely negotiating terms on both sides. Copies of these documents were given to me from a private source.

A Reading List

Many of the books relating to the life of Michael Collins are now out of print but they are available in most public libraries.

Rex Taylor's *Michael Collins* (1958) is a well researched, comprehensive account of his life and times.

Margery Forester's *Michael Collins, The Lost Leader* (1971) is a very powerful piece of writing and all round is probably the best account of the man.

The Big Fellow (1965) by Frank O'Connor is also very good in that it gives a creative writer's insight into the complexities of his life.

Piaras Beaslai's *Michael Collins and the Making of a New Ireland* (1926) is still very worthwhile reading even though a lot of new information has come to light since it was written. Incidentally in one of the files of the Mulcahy Papers now in the U.C.D. Archives there is a large type-written manuscript of comments on this book.

Desmond Ryan's *Michael Collins and the Invisible Army* (1977) is an excellent fictionalised account of his life and adventures.

A recent book by T. Ryle Dwyer, *Michael Collins and the Treaty: His Differences with de Valera,* is excellent.

There are, of course, several other books on Michael Collins, as well as many dealing with the history of the period, but if the reader refers to those mentioned here he will obtain a fairly good insight into most aspects of the life of this extraordinary man.

EPILOGUE:
Did Sonny O'Neill Shoot Michael Collins?

As I write these lines in the autumn of 1990 the mystery of Michael Collins death is more confused than ever. Who shot him and how he met his end is still shrouded in mystery, and there is not even a light showing at the end of the tunnel.

This, of course, is almost entirely the fault of the Free State government who, on the eve of Fianna Fáil coming to power, burned thousands of sensitive documents including a number of files on the shooting of Michael Collins and who, in an extraordinary act of cover-up, refused to hold an inquest into his death despite the strong pressure of people like Major General Seán Hales. Why there was such a massive cover-up has never been satisfactorily explained. The general public have been left puzzled, but in their own shrewd way they know that there must be some compelling reason for this.

Speculation has continued as to who did shoot Michael Collins. Since the last edition of this book a television programme made by RTÉ and two books have suggested that a local IRA man, Denis 'Sonny' O'Neill was the man who shot Collins.These endeavours have, in one sense, been positive developments. It is in the public interest that Collins' death be probed and the results of such investigations be put into the public arena.

However, it is equally in the public interest that any investigations in turn be held up to critical scrutiny.

In my view I find it most unwise to make allegations that cannot stand up to the laws of evidence which apply in any civilised court. Here I propose to look at some of the items put forward as evidence that Sonny O'Neill was the man.

Another element which has added to the confusion has

been the amount of hearsay evidence in circulation, hardly any of it worth a second thought. 'I was always told So-and-So shot him', 'I knew a cousin of one of the survivors who told me', 'a third cousin once removed told me', 'Dubhairt bean liom go ndubhairt bean lei' etc. etc. More than a score of people have named to me one particular man (not Sonny O'Neill) as Collins' killer. Virtually all of this is worthless as real evidence

These rumours have given birth to a number of folktales on who shot Collins, each one as ridiculous as the other. Sensible and solid people have sworn to me that De Valera shot him. Others were equally adamant that he was shot by John McPeake. Still others were quite sure that he was shot by Emmet Dalton. The late Jim Hurley was deeply perturbed by the number of false rumours naming him. Because of the cover-up these stories abound and they surface every few years, hold the stage a little while, and then vanish.

By way of an aside here I should say that when I decided to examine this new *dernier cri* carefully I approached some of Sonny O'Neill's living relations and asked them for their co-operation. At the outset, however, I made it crystal clear to them that if I found the slightest piece of solid evidence implicating him in the shooting I would not hesitate to say so. They willingly agreed to this condition and gave me all the information I asked for.

The first piece of 'evidence' is a letter written to me by the late Máire Comerford shortly before her death. As she was in advanced years at the time it is rather a confused letter. In this letter she says that John Dowling, a Dublin IRA officer, *told* her that Sonny O'Neill *told* him that it was he fired the fatal shot, and she in turn *told* me. Please note the number of times 'told' is used. This is not even hearsay evidence. It is hearsay evidence *three times* removed and as such is worthless. To add to this clumsy uncertainty Máire added; *O'Neill may or may not be his name.'* So it could be anybody. She was not even sure of the name.

I later discussed this whole matter with John Dowling and he was by no means clear as to what happened. He most certainly did *not* say that Sonny O'Neill admitted to firing the fatal shot. He had a vague recollection that some officers of the Dublin Staff of the IRA, whose names he could not remember, had a discussion with a man (unnamed) who *thought* he might have shot Collins. He had no personal interview with this individual himself. Dowling was also in advanced years and his memory was fuzzy when I spoke to him. To show how confused he was – he was quite adamant that Sir John Lavery did not paint the portrait of Collins lying in state and that he merely took a death mask. Both of these statements are false. Lavery *did* paint the portrait of Collins dead and it was the sculptor Albert Power who made the death mask. False also was his insistence that the back of Collins head was not blown away. I consequently did not make any use of Dowling's information as I felt that, even with the best will in the world, his memory could not be relied upon.

I cannot help feeling puzzled as to why Sonny O'Neill would travel to Dublin and tell a number of IRA officers that he was guilty of shooting Collins and at the same time forget to mention this to his own superiors and comrades in West Cork. This simply does not make sense. As evidence this whole incident is worthless and would not be accepted by any court.

Some few months ago a Mr Jim Kearney from Bandon made a number of statements to the effect that: 1) He was one of the four or five who attacked the Collins column and 2) He knew Sonny O'Neill's bullet shot Collins. When I was researching this book I interviewed all known survivors with the exception of John O'Callaghan. These included amongst others Dan Holland, Jim Hurley, Tom Kelleher. As well I interviewed Liam Deasy and Pat Buttimer and not one of them ever mentioned a Mr Jim Kearney being present. They did mention a Mr Pete Kearney, who was present at

Béalnabláth but did not take part in the ambush. During the war I shared living quarters with both Deasy and Buttimer and I discussed the ambush with them many times. I am not saying that Mr Kearney is making misleading statements. What I am saying is that I have no corroborative evidence that he took part in the actual ambush.

In my view the most important man at Béalnabláth from the point of view of a writer was a man called Tom Foley. He could hardly be called an active participant since he was only sixteen years of age at the time and was unarmed. He was in fact the runner. His job was to go for messages, cigarettes etc., to the shop and to bring tea and bread from the local farmers. Because of this he knew the *exact* location of every participant and who they were. A few months before his accidental death he made a tape recording of his memories of that day in Béalnabláth. He was questioned by a local priest on tape. He was absolutely emphatic *that there was no Jim Kearney present amongst those who took part in the ambush.* Furthermore he confirmed what was generally believed that Sonny O'Neill had *left the ambush site* with the main body an hour before the action. This latter evidence was confirmed by Cormac Mac Carthaigh, one of the greatest experts on the death of Collins. He had evidence that O'Neill and some other IRA men were having supper in a safe house about three miles away at the exact time of the ambush. I made an appointment with him to get details of this but unfortunately he died unexpectedly two days before I was to see him.

So here you have totally conflicting statements as to who took part in the ambush. According to Tom Foley neither Sonny O'Neill or Jim Kearney took part in the actual ambush. According to Jim Kearney both himself and Sonny O'Neill were present.

In an attempt to clarify the issue I wrote the following letter to the *Cork Examiner* which was published on 28 September, 1989:

SIR – In your issue of September 18, you report a Mr

Jim Kearney claiming to have taken part in the ambush at Béalnabláth. When I was researching my book *The Shooting of Michael Collins* I interviewed at great length the survivors of the actual ambush, Tom Kelleher and Jim Hurley. They gave me the names of those who took part in the ambush and they never mentioned the name of any Kearney being present.

I also interviewed Liam Deasy who discussed the action in great detail with me. Again there was no mention of any Kearney.

Mr Kearney states he was one of the engineers laying the mines. Jim Hurley and Tom Kelleher both told me that a man named O'Callaghan dismantled one mine which had been laid earlier that day. Hurley helped O'Callaghan. There was no mention of any Kearney.

In the interest of historical accuracy I would be grateful if Mr Kearney could furnish details to substantiate his claims.

JOHN M. FEEHAN

Unfortunately there was no reply to this letter published. Later that month the family of the late Tom Kelleher wrote, *inter alia,* in *The Southern Star:*

Colm Connolly who compiled and presented the documentary on the death of Collins has cast doubts on the involvement of the man he presented in his programme as the last survivor of the ambush at Béalnabláth. On a radio programme presented by Andy O'Mahony August 1989 Colm Connolly stated that he had interviewed people on both sides in the Civil War but only one person could state that Jim Kearney was present when Michael Collins was killed and that person was Jim Kearney himself... If the maker of a programme has doubts about the involvement of a man whom he uses as a major witness then it must be considered unwise and foolhardy to name a particular person as the one who shot Michael Collins.

This letter was published in the *Southern Star* on 3 February 1990 and in this case also no reply has appeared.

The statements therefore given by Mr Kearney cannot be regarded as clear-cut evidence unless he gives some solid substantial proof that he was in fact present at the ambush.

So looking at all the facts there is no conclusive evidence whatever to suggest that Sonny O'Neill was even present at the ambush let alone to say that he fired the fatal shot. What is put forward as evidence is unsubstantiated.

The 'So-and-So told me' school of history, while highly amusing at times, is notoriously unreliable. Interviews with people are only as valuable as the veracity or memory of the person concerned. In themselves they are worthless as evidence and to be of any value would need to be backed up by corroborative evidence of much more solid proportions.

I have had interviews with what appeared to be sound solid people who told me on the highest authority that De Valera shot Collins, that Dalton shot Collins, that McPeake shot Collins and one even told me that Collins was shot in Bandon and he claimed to have seen it happen as a child. These foolish claims are now added to by what appears to be the equally foolish claim that Sonny O'Neill shot Collins.

The reality is that *nobody* knows who shot Collins, and there is *no* solid evidence to show who did.

What we really know about Collins' death can be summarised briefly:

1. Collins was shot by a bullet from a Mauser type pistol which entered his forehead and tore out the whole of one side of his head. He was not shot by a ricochet or a dumdum bullet. A ricochet would make a small gash about 1" - 2" long, and the bullet would remain inside. In so far as my researches show the IRA Chief-of-Staff Liam Lynch had earlier issued explicit verbal instructions to all Republican forces not to use dum-dum bullets under any circum-

132

stances. It is unlikely that those at Béalnabláth would have disobeyed this order. Again none of the participants whom I interviewed ever suggested to me that dum-dums were used. A dum-dum would make a circular wound of about 1" in diameter and the bullet would also remain inside. No such wound was found on Collins. Almost the entire back of his head was blown away and *no bullet whatever was found inside Collins' head*. The only known bullet that would make a small entry wound and then a big gash as an exit wound is from a Mauser type pistol and it is with such a bullet Collins was killed. Several reliable witnesses, including Oliver St. John Gogarty, confirmed the existence of a small entry wound on the forehead.

2. Who fired the bullet we do not know. It was certainly not Sonny O'Neill or De Valera or John McPeake. Strangely enough Emmet Dalton in an interview with Cormac Mac Carthaigh freely admitted that he *could* have shot Collins accidentally. That of course does not say that he did so. But in a last analysis there is no real evidence to show who fired the fatal shot – whether Free State or IRA, and such evidence will not become available unless his body is exhumed. Even now this could confirm once and for all whether the shot was fired by the IRA, 150 yards away, or by the escort, 10 or 15 yards away.

3. Immediately after Collins death there was a massive cover-up by the government. There was no inquest although in the papers of the time reports of inquests on soldiers shot were almost a daily occurrence. There was no enquiry, no proper independent autopsy and almost every document relating to Collins' death is missing. Perhaps the most extraordinary part of this is the affair of the cap in the museum. This cap is not Collins' cap. It is two sizes too small for him. It could not have shrunk over the years as military caps are reinforced inside by steel. Furthermore if military caps shrank after every wetting then the army would have to purchase thousands of these

caps every year to replace the wet ones. My old army cap has been drenched scores of times, has fallen into rivers, lakes, bog-holes and has still retained its size after 35 years of inactivity.

The cap in the museum had a red stain which was supposed to look like blood. Blood stains turn black after a short time so it has been suggested the red is most likely a daub of paint put on to look like blood. There is a tear in the back of the cap to make it look as if it were torn by a bullet, but it is an extraordinary thing that no government had the cap forensically examined for blood stains or powder marks. That surely should have been done before the cap was ever put on public display in the museum. But I am reliably informed that it still could be forensically examined and could still yield valuable information. Is it vain to hope that this may yet be done? In an interview with Cormac Mac Carthaigh, Emmet Dalton expressed the view that the cap was most likely his. But what of the alleged paint and tear at the back? Collins' real cap was given to Cosgrave by Major General Seán Hales as evidence that Collins did not meet his death by a ricochet, and unfortunately, it has vanished.

I again and again want to reiterate the necessity for absolute caution in accepting the 'So-and-So told me' method. The real test of a good writer is how that writer *interprets* what has been said – the vital question here is: *What other known facts corroborate what has been said?* Let me give a final example of how unbelievably nonsensical such interpretations can be. Some commentators believe that Liam Deasy planned the ambush and stayed there all day going around discussing the situation with the men. Nothing could be further from the truth. It was Tom Hales who planned the ambush and Deasy had never been at the site. He spent the entire day three miles away in Gurranereagh attending to correspondence and other Divisional matters.

But let Deasy speak for himself. In his book *Brother Against Brother* he details what happened that day. This is

Deasy's only public statement on Béalnabláth. (My comments in italics.)

That evening(22 August) when we had completed the matters which needed attention Crofts and I left Gurranereagh and walked the three miles to Béalnabláth arriving there about 7 p.m. (*So he had been all day away.*) Jerh Long told us that the column was in ambush position and I walked down the Bandon road in that direction. There I met Tom Hales who was standing in the middle of the road. He told me that as the men had been in such an uncomfortable position all day and as the convoy was not likely to return this way he was giving an order to withdraw. He ordered the Battalion Engineer to remove the mine and detailed some members of the column to remain in position as a protective party while this was being done. About twelve men of the column left in the direction of Newcestown, while others, with Tom Hales and myself walked back along the road to Béalnabláth Cross. (*Here it is important to note that Hales had left the ambush site and gone back with Deasy and others to the pub. Incidentally Pat Buttimer was one of those who moved towards Newcestown and did not take part in the ambush. He has confirmed this on a tape made some years before his death. According to Tom Foley, the runner, Sonny O'Neill left with this group also.*) After such a long tiring day it was only natural that they should have a drink in Long's pub. We were in the pub about ten minutes when we heard the sound of machine-gun and rifle fire coming from the direction of the ambush position. We rushed out to a higher road, the old Béalnabláth-Bandon road, which ran parallel to the lower road. (*It is important to note here that they all left Long's pub and ran along the higher road, including Tom Hales. Deasy's information to me was that they were armed with rifles.*)

135

We crossed a few fields and then came in sight of the ambush position. We had come very quickly and it had not taken us more than fifteen minutes since hearing the first shots. From where we were, some three hundred yards from the actual position, we could see very little – just a lorry and the turret of the armour car with a few soldiers darting from one position to another. We had fired a few shots when suddenly the whole convoy moved off. Later on we were joined by the covering party at the ambush site, who reported that as far as they knew there were no casualties on either side...

Now this latter sentence is most important. If Jim Kearney was one of the covering party present why did he not speak and say that he knew Collins was shot? If Sonny O'Neill was one of the covering party who was alleged to have boasted 'felling' two, why did he not speak up? Deasy is quite explicit. He says the 'covering party'. He does not say *some* of them. This of course raises major questions as to who actually were the covering party.

Further on in that chapter Deasy lists the names of the officers who attended the meeting at Murray's house just after the ambush. It includes Jim Hurley, Dan Holland, Tom Kelleher. Missing from this list are the names of Sonny O'Neill and Jim Kearney. This naturally raises the particular question: Where was Sonny O'Neill? Was he still in the safe house miles away?

Now I have given this incident as an example of how absolutely necessary it is to check and re-check all known facts. Here Deasy publicly tells what happened yet it is astonishing how many commentators never seemed to have checked this statement with what 'somebody told them'. I want to make it clear that in this book I am not making any imputation against anybody. I am merely making a plea for caution in public statements, and for clarification and corroboration in the interests of historical accuracy.

Another suggestion that has been made is that before he died Sonny O'Neill wanted to make friends with the Collins family and at least speak to them. He is supposed to have expressed this wish to Tom Hales but died rather suddenly before he could do so.

This suggestion I find difficult to understand. Sonny O'Neill died in 1950. His brother Jackie, who was an LDF intelligence officer in West Cork during the Emergency, died in May 1944. I was stationed in Collins Barracks, Cork at the time and I went to Jackie's funeral representing the army. I was accompanied in the car by Tom Barry.

We arrived at the O'Neill house in Gaggin and after having paid our respect to the remains upstairs we were brought into a large sitting-room downstairs for refreshments. This sitting-room was crowded, mostly with old IRA men. Sitting together chatting in a most friendly way were *Sonny O'Neill and Johnny Collins, Michael Collins' brother,* The two of them talked away for the best part of two hours until the remains were removed from the house.

I find it extremely difficult to understand how six years later Sonny O'Neill would want to 'break the ice' with Johnny Collins – talk to him – when he had already done so. This just does not make sense.

Every writer makes mistakes, and sometimes believes people who should not be believed. It is simply a professional hazard that goes with the job. But when it comes to accusing a man of committing a murder then there is no room for mistakes or errors, and, because those Republicans who shot at Collins that day were taking part in an act of rebellion against the elected government the shooting of Collins was in strict legal terms, an act of murder if they were responsible. Every detail must be such as to stand up to the most rigorous cross-examination in accordance with the established laws of evidence in any respectable court of law. If that criteria is not measured up to then there is no evidence. Such is the case with Sonny O'Neill. There is no   acceptable evidence to suggest that he was the man who shot Collins. Neither is there any such evidence to suggest any of the others who have been named are guilty. Until there is I respectfully suggest that those who write keep their silence until they have real proof. May I conclude by quoting an extract from a letter written to the papers by Mr Liam Collins, Solicitor, nephew of Michael Collins:

> I would appeal to all to cease for once and for all making his death an emotive, and as it seems clear, hurtful issue to some very decent honourable persons here in my native West Cork and further afield... Alas a bullet from some-one's gun ended my uncle's life. I point a finger at no participant and regret very sincerely that others have chosen to do so.

With those noble and charitable sentiments all decent people must surely agree.

More Interesting Books

THE PATH TO FREEDOM
MICHAEL COLLINS

Many books have been written about the life and death of Michael Collins. *The Path to Freedom* is the only book he wrote himself.

These articles and speeches, first published in 1922, throw light not only on the War of Independence, the Civil War and the foundation of the Free State but on crucial contemporary issues.

> The actions taken indicated an over-keen desire for peace, and although terms of truce were virtually agreed upon, they were abandoned because the British leaders thought their actions indicated weakness, and they consequently decided to insist upon the surrender of our arms. The result was the continuance of the struggle.

Michael Collins on efforts to bring about a truce earlier in 1920.

MICHAEL COLLINS
THE MAN WHO WON THE WAR
T. RYLE DWYER

In formally proposing the adoption of the Anglo-Irish Treaty on 19 December 1921 Arthur Griffith referred to Michael Collins as 'the man who won the War', much to the annoyance of the Defence Minister Cathal Brugha, who questioned whether Collins 'had ever fired a shot at any enemy of Ireland'.

Who was this Michael Collins, and what was his real role in the War of Independence? How was it that two sincere, selfless individuals like Griffith and Brugha, could differ so strongly about him?

This is the story of a charismatic rebel who undermined British morale and inspired Irish people with exploits, both real and imaginary. He co-ordinated the sweeping Sinn Féin election victory of 1918, organised the IRA, set up the first modern intelligence network, masterminded a series of prison escapes and supervised the fundraising to finance the movement.

Collins probably never killed anybody himself, but he did order the deaths of people standing in his way, and even advocated kidnapping an American President. He was the prototype of the urban terrorist and the real architect of the Black and Tan War.

THE GREAT IRISH FAMINE
EDITED BY CATHAL PÓIRTÉIR

This is the most wide-ranging series of essays ever published on the Great Irish Famine and will prove of lasting interest to the general reader. Leading historians, economists, geographers – from Ireland, Britain and the United States – have assembled the most up-to-date research from a wide spectrum of disciplines, including medicine, folklore and literature, to give the fullest account yet of the background and consequences of the Famine.

THE COURSE OF IRISH HISTORY
EDITED BY T. W. MOODY AND F. X. MARTIN

This book provides a rapid short survey, with geographical introduction, of the whole course of Ireland's history. Based on a series of television programmes, it is designed to be both popular and authoritative, concise but comprehensive, highly selective but balanced and fair-minded, critical but constructive and sympathetic. A distinctive feature is its wealth of illustrations.

The present edition is a revised and enlarged version of the original book. New material has been added, bringing the narrative to the IRA ceasefire of 31 August 1994.

BOBBY SANDS AND THE TRAGEDY OF NORTHERN IRELAND
JOHN M. FEEHAN

Bobby Sands captured the imagination of the world when, despite predictions, he was elected a Member of Parliament to the British House of Commons while still on hunger-strike in the Northern Ireland concentration camp of Long Kesh.

– When he later died after sixty-six gruelling days of hunger he commanded more television, radio and newspaper coverage than the papal visits or royal weddings.

– What was the secret of this young man who set himself against the might of an empire and who became a microcosm of the whole northern question and a moral catalyst for the southern Irish conscience?

– In calm, restrained language John M. Feehan records the life of Bobby Sands with whom he had little sympathy in the beginning – though this was to change. At the same time he gives us an illuminating and crystal-clear account of the terrifying statelet of Northern Ireland and of the fierce guerrilla warfare that is turning Northern Ireland into Britain's Vietnam.

THE SECRET PLACES
OF THE
BURREN

JOHN M. FEEHAN

John M. Feehan searches out the hidden corners of the Burren, those secluded places where time stands still and where nature speaks its secret language to the human spirit.

Although at times controversial, cutting through sham and pretence wherever he meets it, he writes with great charm, skill and sympathy, and with a deep love of the countryside and its people.

He sees the mystery, the beauty and the sense of wonder in ordinary things and brings each situation to life so that the reader feels almost physically present.

This is a most delightful Irish travel book that can be read again and again.

MY VILLAGE
MY WORLD

JOHN M. FEEHAN

This is a book that never palls or drags. It is boisterous and ribald and I am tempted to say that it is by far the funniest book I have ever read. It is also an accurate and revealing history of rural Ireland half a century ago and more. John M. Feehan writes beautifully throughout. I love this book.

From the Foreword by JOHN B. KEANE

My Village – My World is a fascinating account of ordinary people in the countryside. It depicts a way of life that took thousands of years to evolve and mature and was destroyed in a single generation. As John M. Feehan says 'Nobody famous ever came from our village. None of its inhabitants ever achieved great public acclaim ... The people of our village could be described in government statistics as unskilled. That would be a false description. They were all highly skilled, whether in constructing privies or making coffins, digging drains or cutting hedges, droving cattle or tending to stallions ... I do not want to paint a picture of an idyllic village like Goldsmith's phony one. We had our sinners as well as our saints ...'